Woodwork

Questions and Answers books are available on the following subjects:

Amateur Radio
Automobile Brakes & Braking
Automobile Electrical Systems
Automobile Engines
Automobile Steering &
Suspension
Automobile Transmission
Systems
BASIC Programming
Brickwork & Blockwork
Cameras
Car Body Care & Repair
Car Maintenance
Carpentry & Joinery
CB Radio
Central Heating
Colour Television
Cycles & Cycling
Diesel Engines
Domestic Lighting
Electric Arc Welding
Electric Motors
Electric Wiring
Electricity
Electronics
Gas Shielded Arc Welding
Gas Welding & Cutting

Gems
GRP Boat Construction
Hi-Fi
Home Insulation
Home Plumbing
Household Security
Integrated Circuits
Lathework
Light Commercial Vehicles
Microprocessors
Motorcycles
Motoring Breakdowns
Painting & Decorating
Personal Computing
Pipework & Pipewelding
Plastering
Plumbing
Radio & Television
Radio Repair
Refrigeration
Steel Boat Construction
Transistors
Video
Videocassette Recorders
Wooden Boat Construction
Woodwork
Yacht & Boat Design

QUESTIONS & ANSWERS

Woodwork

Gordon Warr

Newnes Technical Books

Newnes Technical Books

is an imprint of the Butterworth Group
which has principal offices in
London, Boston, Durban, Singapore, Sydney, Toronto, Wellington

First published 1984

© Butterworth & Co (Publishers) Ltd, 1984

British Library Cataloguing in Publication Data

Warr, Gordon
  Woodwork.—(Questions & answers)
  1. Woodwork—Examinations, questions, etc.
  I. Title   II. Series
  684'.08'076   TT185

  ISBN 0-408-01405-9

Library of Congress Cataloging in Publication Data

Warr, Gordon.
  Woodwork.
  (Questions & answers)
  Includes index.
  1. Woodwork.   I. Title.   II. Series.
  TT180.W342 1984   684'.08   83-23614
  ISBN 0-408-01405-9

Photoset by Butterworths Litho Preparation Department
Printed in England by Whitstable Litho Ltd, Whitstable, Kent

Preface

Woodworking is one of the oldest of crafts, and is widely practised in many specialised aspects as well as the more familiar ones of joinery and furniture making. Wood is the most versatile of all our raw materials, which probably explains why demand for it is continuing to rise.

For the home woodworker, opportunities for pursuing this craft have never been better. Power tools of all types are in abundance, with sizes and types to suit all needs and pockets, and there has never been a better range of hardware on the market. Timber yards are well stocked, even if some hardwoods may take a little searching for, and man-made boards of all types can be bought by amateurs as readily as professionals. The growth of DIY outlets in recent years means that woodworkers can often obtain all their materials and tools locally.

Woodworking is such a diverse subject that the number of questions which can be asked is vast. This book inevitably contains only a relatively small selection of these, with the answers aimed at providing as much background information as possible under the general label of 'basic woodworking'.

G.W.

Contents

1
Timber and man-made boards

Timber

What are the main parts of a tree, and why is the heartwood normally preferred to the sapwood?

The main parts of a tree are shown in Fig. 1. With the vast majority of trees, growth takes place in the cambium layer. With tropical timbers the annual rings tend to be less distinct than with trees from the temperate and colder regions of the world. This is because of the marked difference in the seasonal climatic conditions which are reflected in the tree's growth. This is seen in the pronounced annual rings, the lighter and wider band being the spring growth, and the darker, narrower ring being the summer growth.

The sapwood is the newer wood of the tree, and as the name suggests carries the sap, or foodstuffs, first from the roots to the leaves. Here the action of the sunlight converts the sap into a usable form, when it passes down the tree to be used for growth. As new wood is added under the bark, the inner part of the sapwood matures into heartwood. The heartwood is the oldest part of the tree, and is preferred because it is both denser and more stable. In addition, the colour is usually richer than that of the sapwood, and is better able to resist rot, fungal attack, and infestation from various beetles. The actual heart, though, is best avoided.

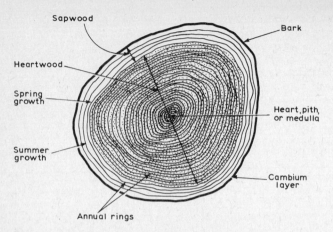

Fig. 1. Section through a tree trunk

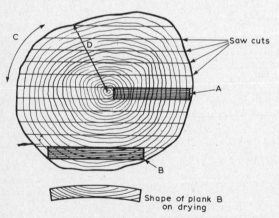

Fig. 2. A. Radial plank; B. Tangential plank; C. Circumferential shrinkage; D. Radial shrinkage

What are the principal differences between hardwoods and softwoods?

There is one fundamental difference. The distinction is a botanical one, being the type of tree which yields the wood. All trees are either deciduous or coniferous. Deciduous trees usually have broad leaves which are shed in winter, and these trees give us the hardwoods. Coniferous means cone-bearing; these trees normally have needle-like leaves and they are in-leaf throughout the year, and because of this are also known as evergreens. These trees yield softwoods. There are certain exceptions to the above.

Generally, hardwoods are slow-growing and tend to be hard and dense. Softwoods tend to grow fast, and are generally lighter and softer. Whereas softwoods are usually pale in colour, hardwoods are of widely different colours from near-white of holly, through browns, reds, greenish and yellowish hues, to ebony which can be jet-black.

What is the usual method of converting timber, and what are 'radial' and 'tangential' boards?

The commonest method of converting the log is by sawing 'through and through', as shown in Fig. 2. This is also known as 'slab' or 'slash' sawing. This is the most economical method of conversion, and results in planks with differing grain characteristics.

Fig. 2A shows a radial plank, with the annual rings running approximately at right angles to the face. B is a tangential plank, with the rings roughly parallel to the face. When timber dries it also shrinks, but the shrinkage is not uniform in all directions. Lengthways it is so slight it can be ignored. Circumferential shrinkage, shown by arrow C, is quite considerable, and is about double the radial shrinkage indicated by arrow D. It is this unequal shrinkage which causes the wood to warp and distort, and in some cases the splits and cracks.

A radial plank or board will shrink, but remain flat. A tangential plank or board will have a tendency to cup away from the heart. In timbers with strong medullary rays such as oak, these will show themselves in a far more pronounced way in radial boards. Such timber is known as 'quartered' or 'figured'.

What are the different methods of seasoning timber, and how dry should the timber be before it is used?

The two methods of seasoning, or drying, timber are natural and by kiln. The former is also known as air drying, while the use of a kiln is often described as kilning, or artificial seasoning. In natural drying, the timber is stacked clear of the ground, with the planks spaced out and separated by strips of wood known as 'stickers'. The stack is best under cover, but with plenty of air circulation. The method is slow, taking approximately one year for each 25 mm (1 in) of thickness of the plank.

With kiln drying, the timber is stacked as before, usually on some kind of trolley, so that it can be wheeled into the kiln chamber in which it is then sealed. By controlling the heat, humidity and air circulation, the time for drying is reduced to a few weeks. Some modern kilns work on a vacuum principle, when drying can be completed in a matter of days.

Timber is never reduced to complete dryness. Being hygroscopic, it absorbs moisture when the surrounding humidity is high, and releases moisture under dry conditions. The amount of moisture in timber is described as the 'moisture content' (MC), and this is expressed as a percentage of its weight if completely dry.

This is why an outside door often 'sticks' in the wetter months of winter, as absorption of moisture results in swelling. In the drier part of the year, the fit of the door is satisfactory. It is also the reason why when wood is used in fairly wide widths, the construction must allow for the wood to swell and shrink slightly according to the humidity of its surroundings. Examples of allowing for what is known as the 'movement' of timber are in table tops, and traditional panelling.

Ideally, for furniture the MC should be around 6–8 per cent. For joinery, a MC of 10–15 per cent is satisfactory, while for construction work the MC can be as high as 25 per cent.

What is meant by 'secondary seasoning'?

Because timber adjusts to the humidity of the environment, timber stored in sheds is rarely likely to have a low enough MC for furniture and good-quality joinery work. It helps, therefore, if timber can be stored indoors for a few weeks prior to its use, ideally where there is gentle heating, so that the timber can be seasoned to indoor conditions. This is known as secondary seasoning, and such timber should be stored flat so as to prevent distortion.

What is meant by 'green' timber?

This has nothing to do with its colour. It refers to timber which has been freshly felled, or which is only partly seasoned. Timber which still has a very high MC is said to be green.

What are the common faults in timber?

These include the following:

(a) Cupping. This is where a plank or board becomes curved across its width (Fig. 3). The nearer the plank originally was to the outside of the tree, the more prone it is to cupping. The cupping is away from the heart, and is allied to drying and shrinkage.

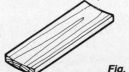

Fig. 3. Cupping

(b) Bowing. This is where a piece of timber becomes curved in its length, and is invariably due to poor stacking during seasoning (Fig. 4).

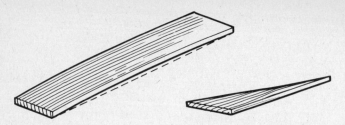

Fig. 4. *Bowing*   **Fig. 5.** *Twisted plank*

(c) Twist. This is illustrated in Fig. 5, and like all forms of distortion is the result of the internal stresses in the timber becoming out of equilibrium, and this is usually during the seasoning process.

It is virtually impossible to straighten a distorted piece of wood. It is better to cut it into smaller pieces, and then plane out the fault. Pieces which are relatively short and narrow will have proportionally much less distortion in them.

(d) Knots. These are where branches have originated within the trunk, and may be live or dead. A live knot is one where the fibres are well integrated with those of the surrounding wood. A dead knot is one where there is no such anchorage, and therefore such a knot can literally 'drop out' leaving a 'knot hole'. Large knots in timber should be avoided as they can seriously weaken timber where strength is important. Small knots usually have to be tolerated, especially in most species of softwood.

(e) Waney edge. This is where the original curved outer surface of the log, with or without the bark, is still retained after cutting to plank or board. The fault is caused by attempting to cut the timber too economically, and is shown in Fig. 6. Sometimes one or both edges of a plank are deliberately left waney for decorative purposes.

(f) Shakes and splits. These are fissures in the timber. Splits take place along the grain, and are commonest at the ends. Again this is connected with drying and associated shrinkage. Because of the

6

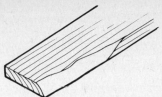

Fig. 6. *Waney edge*

cellular nature of timber, moisture is more readily lost through the ends of a plank, than through it sides and edges. Often the ends of a plank are painted or otherwise sealed to prevent the too rapid loss of moisture from these surfaces during seasoning.

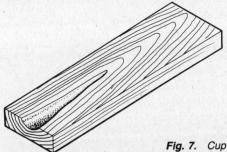

Fig. 7. *Cup shake*

A *cup shake* is where the annual rings become separated. Often this results in the fault shown in Fig. 7, where the consequence of the shake is that a small piece of wood becomes completely detached. A *thunder shake* is a fissure which goes across the grain, and can result in the complete failure of the timber if subjected to a load or strain.

What is meant by plank, board, scantling, and square?

The expressions plank and board have similar and overlapping meanings, and their usage varies a little in different parts of the country, and in different branches of woodworking. The generally accepted interpretation of a plank is a piece of wood over around 38 mm (1½ in) thick, while a board is a piece up to this thickness.

Scantlings are lengths of timber of relatively small section, say up to around 75 mm × 100 mm (3 in × 4 in). Squares are lengths of timber which are square in section.

What are the differences between carcassing quality and joinery quality?

Carcassing quality is a term used to describe a softwood used for constructional and similar purposes, such as floor joists and roofing members, fencing, and pallets. The timber often includes a lot of knots and sapwood, and frequently the seasoning is limited. The species or grades employed for carcassing are those which cannot be used for better-class work, and they are nearly always used with sawn surfaces only. Two common species used for carcassing are hemlock and whitewood.

The accepted timber for softwood joinery is redwood, or red deal. Joinery quality therefore refers to this species, selected for its superiority in freedom from large knots and absence of sapwood. Fairly close annual rings are also a desirable feature, and joinery quality also implies it is suitably seasoned.

What is meant by the machining allowance?

The sizes which are used to describe a piece of wood are those to which the timber is initially sawn. Such timber when planed will therefore finish less than the sawn sizes. Thus, for example, 50 mm × 100 mm (2 in × 4 in) sawn stock will actually measure this size, but 50 mm × 100 mm planed timber will measure approximately 46 mm × 94 mm. This is still referred to as nominal 50 mm × 100 mm. Around 4 mm (⅙ in) is lost in planing on dimensions up to about 75 mm (3 in), and rather more if the width exceeds this. Planed timber is sometimes referred to as 'dressed' or 'wrot'.

What do the terms PAR, PBS, and P2S mean?

PAR means 'planed all round', that is on both sides and both edges. PBS and P2S have the same meaning, which is 'planed both sides', and 'planed two sides', but not the edges. Softwoods of fairly small section are frequently sold as PAR, also hardwood strips which are often available at DIY outlets. Planing both sides is a more common way of preparing hardwoods, where the widths tend to be 'random', anyway.

What is ready-prepared stock?

This is timber which has been machined so that its sectional profile makes it suitable for particular uses. Because timber so machined is used a lot for joinery-type work, the wood used is nearly always red deal. Common sections include architraves and skirting, handrailing, beads of various shapes, and the various component parts of a window frame. These include sill, mullion, head and stiles, and material for sashes. Ready-prepared stock is likely to vary quite considerably from merchant to merchant; a selection of sections is shown in Fig. 8.

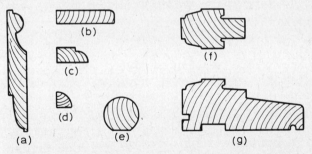

Fig. 8. *Ready-machined stock: (a) reversible skirting, (b) architrave, (c) glazing bead, (d) quadrant, (e) handrail, (f) window mullion, and (g) window sill*

9

Ready-machined stock also includes tongue and groove boarding, Plain T & G is much used for flooring, while T, G & Vee is used for more decorative purposes. The latter is sometimes known as 'match boarding', and can have a finished thickness as little as 10 mm (⅜ in).

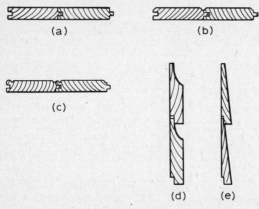

Fig. 9. Ready-machined boarding: (a) plain tongue and groove, (b) tongue, groove and vee, (c) tongue, groove and bead, (d) weather boarding, and (e) ship-lap boarding

Weather boarding is also bought ready-machined, and is usually used as a cladding material on sheds, gable ends, and between ground floor and upper windows especially on those of the 'bay' type. Two common patterns of weather boarding are included in Fig. 9.

What hardwoods are in common use, and what characteristics make them suitable for particular purposes?

Common imported hardwoods include iroko, ramin, mahogany and beech.

Iroko is a tough timber with a fairly irregular and interlocked grain. It is of mid-brown colour, and is highly resistant to rot. It can be obtained in large widths. Because of its durability, it is used for outdoor work, especially garden furniture. It is not used for domestic furniture, but is employed for good-class joinery which is to be given a 'clear' finish.

Ramin is straw-coloured and straight-grained, and is much used for dowel making. It is a fairly hard timber, but is prone to splitting, and is not particularly durable. Ramin is widely available in fairly small sectional sizes of PAR stock, and it is regarded as a 'general-purpose' timber, often used for small-scale work as a substitute for softwood. It looks rather uninteresting if given a clear finish.

Mahogany grows in most of the hot regions of the world, with the result that there are a great number of varieties of this timber. Indeed, almost all reddish-coloured hardwoods are loosely referred to as 'mahoganies'. The grain may be straight or interlocked, with colours ranging from pink to deep red. Mahogany is fairly durable, making it suitable for boat building. It is used for furniture, also hardwood joinery including windows and good-quality entrance doors, especially of the 'traditional' panelled type.

Beech is a tough, hard-wearing timber, with a close straight grain and pale pink in colour. Not suitable for outdoor use because of low resistance to rot, the timber is otherwise widely used for furniture, toys, tool parts, dowels, and hardwood floors. The wood is difficult to split.

Which softwoods are in everyday use?

The most widely used softwood is redwood, or red deal. This timber grows widely in the northern hemisphere, and is sometimes known by its geographical origin, for example, Baltic or Russian redwood. This is the timber used for 'pine' furniture and fitments. It has a pale reddish colouring which darkens with age. Better grades which are free of sapwood are reasonably resistant to rot, but must be treated with a preservative or painted for outdoor use.

Whitewood, or white deal, is off-white in colour and can sometimes be confused with redwood. It is used mostly for carcassing purposes, sheds, flooring, and temporary work. Because it is obtainable in good widths, it's suitable for shelving and fascia boards. An inferior timber to redwood, whitewood often contains knots which can be particularly hard.

Cedar is a Canadian timber of pale reddish-brown, and light weight. Although the timber has only limited strength, it has a natural resistance to rot making it ideal for outdoor use, including garden furniture and roofing shingles ('wooden' slates). Usually it has good straight grain, clear of knots. It is sometimes used for panelling and decorative purposes, its rich colour looking attractive when given a clear finish.

Parana pine is a native of South America. Normally pale in colour, it can have vivid streaks of green, red, and near-black. Obtainable in wide stock clear of knots, it is used for certain parts of joinery work, especially staircases and window bottoms, or boards.

Hemlock is another Canadian timber. It is pinkish in colour with the grain a little woolly in nature. Poorer grades are used for carcassing, better-quality for mass-produced doors. Hemlock can be obtained with good straight grain and freedom from knots, such stock being used for the stiles of ladders.

Man-made boards

What is plywood, and does it shrink and warp?

Ply consists of thin layers of wood, known as the plies, glued together so that the grain of one piece is at right angles to its neighbour. Normally an odd number of plies is used, so that the grain on the outer laminations is running the same way. Because of the way the plies are cut from the log, and the way in which the board is built-up, large sizes, up to 3050 mm × 1525 mm (10 ft × 5 ft) can be made, with individual plies varying from

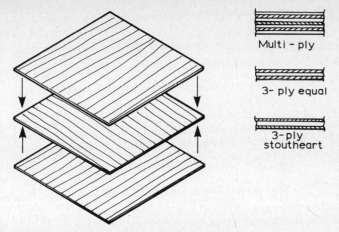

Fig. 10. *The principle of plywood construction*

under half a millimetre (¹⁄₅₀ in), to 3 mm (¹⁄₈ in) in thickness. See Fig. 10.

Plywood does not shrink. Wood only shrinks across the grain, not lengthways. Because of the manner in which the ply is made with the grain running in two directions, it does not shrink or swell, as each lamination prevents adjoining ones from moving.

Although plywood does not warp for the reasons which solid wood does, it will distort under certain conditions. It is in any case fairly flexible.

What are the advantages and disadvantages of plywood compared with solid wood?

Plywood has a number of advantages over solid wood, but also some drawbacks. On the credit side may be listed:

(a) Available in wide sheets, the standard size of a man-made board being 2440 mm × 1220 mm (8 ft × 4 ft).

13

(b) Does not shrink or split.

(c) Faults can be eliminated at the time of manufacture, and minor faults on the surfaces can be patched as the plywood is being made.

(d) For curved work, thin grades can be readily bent with little danger of fracture.

(e) Normally supplied ready-sanded, or at least with surfaces which do not need a lot of further preparation.

(f) Can be obtained ready-veneered in better-quality woods, thus giving the appearance of solid, expensive wood.

(g) The timbers used are seasoned during manufacture, therefore further drying out is not needed.

Disadvantages include the following:

(a) Unsightly edges which normally have to be concealed in some way.

(b) Lengths normally limited to 2440 mm (8 ft).

(c) Jointing methods have to be modified for plywood, which does not lend itself too well to traditional techniques.

(d) Fairly weak if cut into narrow pieces.

(e) Difficult to use nails or screws into the edge of plywood, where there is always some danger that they could force the plies apart.

Can plywood be used out-of-doors?

Most plywoods, for reasons of economy, are manufactured with adhesives which are non-waterproof. Such plywood, however well-protected by paint or other methods, will, if used outside, sooner or later absorb water with the result that de-lamination will occur as the adhesive becomes softened. However, outdoor-grade plywood is made using a waterproof glue, and is stamped to indicate that it is suitable for outdoor use.

A very superior type of waterproof plywood is known as marine grade. This is much used in boat-building work, and for such rigorous use the ply has to be made to a British Standards specification. Marine ply has to withstand 72 hours immersed in boiling water without any signs of the glue weakening. Only high-grade timbers are used for marine plywood, and the whole of the manufacture is to a high standard.

What is faced plywood?

This is plywood which has been veneered with one of the more attractive and expensive woods. However, to veneer only one face of plywood would put the board out-of-balance, and result in it becoming bowed. The veneer has the effect of 'pulling' the sheet, the veneered side becoming the hollow one. Therefore the correct procedure is to veneer both sides to keep the board in balance. Because the reverse side of the ply is often never seen, a 'plain' veneer is usually used on this reverse side, and is known as a 'balancer'. It is possible to obtain plywood with both sides veneered with the same specie of one of the more attractive woods.

What are typical uses of plywood?

Plywood has many uses, and is particularly useful where the width of the sheet can be taken advantage of. In furniture making, it is extensively employed for the backs of units, and the bases of drawers. For joinery, the 'risers' in a flight of stairs are now invariably of plywood. It is also used for panelled work, as a wall-cladding material and in the manufacture of doors. Constructional grades are used for sub-floors, for partitions, and for formwork used in concreting. Plywood is also used in toy making, and box manufacture. Exterior grades can be used for sheds and other wooden buildings, and marine grade for the hulls of boats, and their fitting out.

What are the differences between blockboard, battenboard, and laminboard?

These boards are of similar basic construction. The different names relate to the widths of the strips which make up the core, which is normally of softwood. Blockboard is by far the commonest of the three variations, where the core strips are around 19 mm (¾ in) wide. Battenboard has the core strips around 63 mm–75 mm (2½ in–3 in) wide, making it less expensive. Battenboard can develop slight surface undulations because of the widths of the core strips, but this depends on other factors such as the grain arrangement of the strips, and their seasoning. Laminboard, on the other hand, is a very superior board with the core strips only around 4 mm (³⁄₁₆ in) wide. These are often of the plainer hardwoods, Fig. 11 shows sections through these three boards.

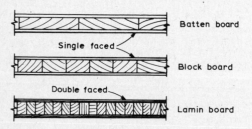

Fig. 11. *Three different types of built-up board*

Note that the facing laminations can be 'single' or 'double' plies, depending on overall quality. These outer laminations are invariably of hardwood, birch being extensively used. Laminboard is usually limited to thicknesses up to 19 mm (¾ in), with blockboard available up to approximately 51 mm (2 in). Laminboard can be veneered as for plywood.

These boards have very varied uses, although to some extent they have been overtaken by chipboard.

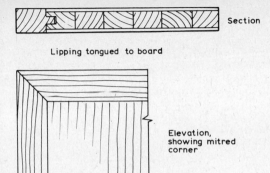

Fig. 12. *Lipping applied to blockboard*

One of the problems with boards with strip cores is the unsightly edges. Fig. 12 shows one of the commonest methods of overcoming the problem, where a piece of wood is tongued to the edge. These pieces are known as 'lippings', and if on a cabinet door or similar would be mitered at the corners.

What are the different types of hardboard which are available?

Hardboard is made from wood pulp, mixed with a bonding agent and subjected to pressure to produce the board. 'Standard' hardboard is of medium density, and has one side smooth and one with indentations. Standard size is 2440 mm × 1220 mm (8 ft × 4 ft), with many others available. Usual thickness is 3 mm (⅛ in), but thicker sizes are also made.

Oil-tempered hardboard contains an additive making it suitable for outdoor use, and it is usually denser than the standard grade. Hardboard with both sides smooth is also made. Perforated hardboard, usually referred to as pegboard, is much used for display purposes, for which a range of fittings have been designed to fit into the holes in the board. There is also a

17

perforated type of hardboard where the board is stamped to give different patterns of a 'fretted' nature. This is a decorative hardboard. White-faced hardboard has its smooth side finished satin-white, and this is extensively used for the backs of furniture, especially kitchen units.

Hardboard is also made with a woodgrain effect, usually produced by a photo-print process which gives a good degree of realism at an economical cost. This is much used for panelling purposes, especially wall panelling.

What is chipboard?

Chipboard is a board manufactured from wood chips and an adhesive, and is also known as particle board. The chips are specially produced from softwoods to different sizes and grades, and for this forest thinnings and branches are usually used. Chipboard is manufactured to different densities according to the pressure used in the presses. It is available with slightly different degrees of surface smoothness, according to the use to which it is to be put. Fire-retardant grades are also made. It is usually manufactured with a non-waterproof adhesive, making it suitable for indoor use only. It can also be obtained with a plastics laminate surface, normally patterned on one side with a white balancer. Panel sizes are as for plywood, with the two popular thicknesses being 13 mm and 19 mm (½ in and ¾ in).

Can chipboard be used for flooring purposes?

A flooring grade of chipboard is made just for this use. It is of fairly high density, and has a thickness of 22 mm (⅞ in). The panels have a nominal size of 2440 mm × 610 mm (8 ft × 2 ft), with one long edge and one end having a tongue formed on them, the other two having corresponding grooves. These panels are now extensively used in house building.

18

What are veneered chipboard panels?

These are panels of board with both sides and two long edges being veneered at the time of manufacture. The panels are made in lengths of 1830 mm (6 ft), and 2440 mm (8 ft), and in widths from 150 mm (6 in) up to 1220 mm (4 ft). Width increments are 76 mm (3 in) up to 915 mm (3 ft). Usual thickness of this product is 16 mm (5/8 in), although both thicker and thinner panels are made.

The most popular veneer used on these panels is mahogany, but they are also available veneered in other woods including pine and teak. With very expensive veneers, mahogany is used on the reverse side as the balancer to keep the costs down.

These panels are also made with a 'melamine' finish. This is a plastic coating which completely covers and seals the chipboard and provides a smooth surface. The melamine may be of a plain colour, usually restricted to white and ivory, or of a simulated woodgrain effect.

Can melamine-faced chipboard panels be used for kitchen worktops?

No. This surface is not sufficiently tough and hard wearing for the rigours of a worktop. Melamine-faced chipboard is ideal for making kitchen units except working surfaces, and is much used for vertical components, shelves and doors. A plastics laminate, or material with similar qualities, should be used for worktops.

Can chipboard be worked with ordinary woodworking tools?

Yes. The material does have different characteristics to solid wood, particularly relating to the grain, but it can be sawn, planed, drilled, screwed and generally worked as wood would be. However, only saws with 'fine' teeth should be used to prevent any 'crumbling' of the material, and planes must be kept sharp for the same reason. It must be remembered, though, that chipboard is fairly abrasive, and therefore planes especially become dulled quickly and must be sharpened frequently. All holes for screws must be pre-drilled. If chipboard is being cut with a circular saw, then blades with teeth of the 'rip-saw' type should be avoided, and preferably a tungsten carbide-tipped blade used.

What is edging veneer?

Edging veneer is a strip of real wood veneer, or thin plastic, used for covering the edges of veneered chipboard panels. Although the panels are produced with the long edges ready-veneered, when they are cut to length the exposed ends need to be covered to conceal the chipboard core. This of course also applies to the long edges if a standard panel has to be cut down in width.

The edging strip is supplied in rolls, with a heat-sensitive adhesive already applied to one side. A domestic iron is used to bond the strip in place, and this needs to be set to 'medium' heat in order to melt the adhesive. Too high a setting will cause scorching of the strip. Even with the iron set at medium heat, it is advisable to have a piece of ordinary brown paper between the iron and the strip to prevent any risk of overheating, and this applies especially to the plastic edging strip. The iron should 'dwell' on the veneer just sufficiently long to melt the adhesive and create the bond.

The strips are manufactured approximately 3 mm (⅛ in) wider than the thickness of the panel, and this excess has to be removed once the veneer is bonded in place. It may be levelled off completely by using glasspaper, or by using an 'edging' trimmer, a plastic-bodied tool housing a blade which cuts away the excess. If using glasspaper to carry out the levelling, the paper must be wrapped around a block, and the direction of working must be 'onto' the board, otherwise damage may be done.

What is 'plastics laminate'?

This is the extremely tough and hard-wearing sheet facing material loosely known as 'Formica', although this is the name of one of the leading manufacturers of this sheeting. It is made from several sheets of paper, impregnated with a special resin, then subjected to very considerable pressure while the resin cures. The pattern is provided by one of the sheets of paper having the design pre-printed on it, although plain colours are also produced.

The usual thickness of plastics laminates is 1.5 mm ($\frac{1}{16}$ in), with a standard sheet size of 2440 mm × 1220 mm (8 ft × 4 ft). Thinner sheets are made, also other sheet sizes. As well as the normal range of patterns, it is also produced in a number of woodgrain effects, and these with a full gloss or satin finish. Also available is a 'super range' of woodgrain plastics, giving an extremely high degree of realism.

How are plastics laminates secured?

Plastics laminate is a facing material which is added to other sheet material such as chipboard, blockboard, and plywood. It is not wise to face solid wood with this material except in narrow pieces, because of the 'movement' of solid wood in wide pieces. It is usually added to its base with an 'impact' adhesive, which provides a strong, waterproof bond with little cramping. Other adhesives can be used provided adequate pressure is applied during setting.

2
Tools and equipment

What is the difference between a marking gauge and a cutting gauge?

A marking gauge has a pointed spur to mark the wood, whereas a cutting gauge has a small blade.

A marking gauge is used to make a line along the wood, that is parallel to the grain, and usually working with the stock of the gauge against the face side or face edge. If a marking gauge is used across the grain, it will scratch the wood because of the directional nature of the fibres making up the grain.

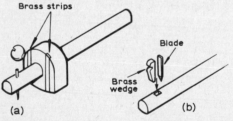

Fig. 13. *(a) Marking gauge, (b) cutting gauge, with blade and brass wedge withdrawn*

A cutting gauge is used across the grain, its blade severing the fibres thus making a clean incision on the surface, rather than a scratch. A cutting gauge can only be properly used if the end of the wood has been trued up, or 'shot'. Fig. 13 shows the two gauges.

What is a sliding bevel used for?

A sliding bevel can be thought of as an adjustable try square, and is therefore used for marking out angles other than 90°. It is also used for testing angles, for example when the edge of a piece of wood is being planed to create a bevel. A sliding bevel can also be used when dovetailing.

When is a marking knife used for marking out, rather than a pencil?

A marking knife is used at the place where the wood is actually going to be cut. For example, a tenon shoulder would be marked out with a knife, and the location of the corresponding mortice in

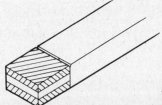

Fig. 14. *Vee-groove formed in waste*

pencil. A marking-knife line is extremely precise but, because it cuts into the wood slightly, cannot be easily removed. The marking knife is also advantageous to use as the start of a 'vee groove', cut by chisel and shown in Fig. 14. A vee groove is a wise preamble where a very accurate cut has to be made by saw, and when the wood is fairly wide.

How does a mortice chisel differ from a paring chisel?

First it must be established that the chisel popularly known as a mortice chisel is more strictly called a registered chisel, and sometimes as a registered mortice chisel. There are a number of differences, all based on the fact that a mortice chisel does relatively heavy work invariably in conjunction with a mallet. Paring chisels are intended for much lighter cuts, usually with only gentle pressure being exerted. Differences include:

(a) The mortice chisel has a much thicker blade, irrespective of its width, compared with a paring chisel. Not only does this add to the strength, it helps to prevent the chisel from 'twisting' in the mortice.

(b) A leather washer is introduced behind the blade 'shoulder' on the mortice chisel. This acts as a shock absorber, cushions the mallet blows, and therefore lessens jarring of the hand.

(c) On the mortice chisel, a ferrule is added to the top of the handle. This is to prevent damage from the constant blows it receives.

(d) The handle is invariably of ash on a mortice chisel, a timber renowned for its resilience. On a paring chisel, ash, beech and box are used, with an increasing number of plastic handles being fitted.

(e) The grinding angle on a mortice chisel is a little steeper than on a paring chisel, as this lessens the chance of damage to the cutting edge.

Fig. 15 shows a mortice chisel.

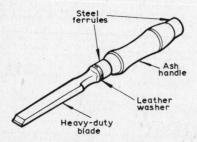

Fig. 15. *Registered pattern mortice chisel*

24

What is a gouge?

A gouge can be thought of as a chisel with the blade curved in its
width. Both the width, and the degree of curvature, vary
considerably. Most important, though, is the sharpening, which
can be on the inside of the curve (in-canalled or canalled), or the
outside (out-canalled). The inside gouge is used for paring
purposes, and the outside gouge for hollowing. Different patterns
of gouges are used for woodturning, and for carving.

What is the best plane to use for general purposes?

Either a jack plane, or a smoothing plane, can be adapted for
general use. Smoothing planes have a length of around 254 mm
(10 in) with blade widths of 45 mm (1¾ in), 50 mm (2 in), and
60 mm (2⅜ in). Jack planes are about 370 mm (14½ in) long,
with blade widths of 50 mm (2 in), or 60 mm (2⅜ in).

However, it is the way these planes are sharpened and adjusted
that determines how they are best suited for different types of
work. For fine shavings, as are needed when 'cleaning-up'
woodwork, the blade should be sharpened with its cutting edge

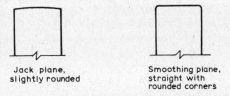

Jack plane,
slightly rounded

Smoothing plane,
straight with
rounded corners

Fig. 16. *Shapes of jack and smoothing-plane blades*

straight, with only the corners rounded to prevent marks being
left on the surface. For heavier planing, as when initially
preparing wood to size, a slightly curved blade is more efficient.
Fig. 16 illustrates the difference.

For fine work, the cap iron should be set very close to the edge
of the blade. Also the mouth of the plane should be reduced to a

25

minimum. This is done by adjusting the 'frog' of the plane, so that the whole of the blade assembly moves forward.

Where thicker shavings need to be removed and the wood trued-up, the efficiency of the plane is at its best if the cap iron is set back about 1.5 mm (1/16 in) from the edge of the blade. When thicker shavings are being removed, the size of the mouth may be increased to allow for this.

If fairly coarse shavings are being removed, the surface produced will be less smooth, and if the grain of the wood is irregular, some tear-out of the grain is very likely to occur.

What are spokeshaves used for?

Spokeshaves are used for smoothing the edges of curved work. A spokeshave is really a sort of plane, so short from front to back that the handles are positioned on the sides. There are two patterns of spokeshave, one where the face is flat, and the other with a round face. The flat-faced spokeshave is used for convex curves, and the round-faced for concave ones. This is shown in Fig. 17, along with the direction of movement in order to be working with the grain.

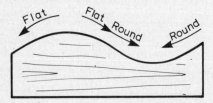

Fig. 17. *Directions of use for spokeshaves*

Spokeshaves are also used in forming decorative chamfers, and were much used in the past on wooden-wheeled carts.

Cheaper versions of spokeshaves have their blade adjusted manually, while better ones have a pair of knurled nuts to control the blade. Some spokeshaves have bodies of cast iron, while others are of malleable iron, which is unbreakable.

What types of bit are available for use in a carpenter's breast brace?

A selection of bits for use in a brace is shown in Fig. 18. The Jennings-type auger bit is a highly efficient tool and is made in a range of sizes up to 38 mm (1½ in). A similar bit is the solid-centre auger bit. Both these bits are excellent for boring deep holes, and in any direction of the grain.

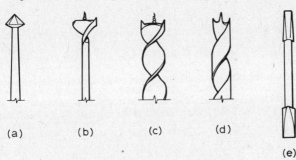

Fig. 18. *Types of bit: (a) countersink, (b) screwnosed, (c) Jennings, (d) lip-and-spur, and (e) double-ended screwdriver*

A somewhat cheaper bit is the screw-nosed centre bit. Again available up to 38 mm (1½ in), this is at its best on shallow holes or thinnish material, but less efficient on end grain.

A Forstner bit is more specialised, its tiny point only being used at the start, after which the cutting is controlled by the rim of the tool. It is used for shallow and overlapping holes.

For large holes, expanding bits are available. These will cut up to 76 mm (3 in), but at this size require a lot of physical effort to rotate.

Countersinks for use in a brace can be either of the snail pattern with a single cutting edge, or the rose variety, with multiple cutters.

Although not used for boring holes, screwdriver bits can be obtained for fitting into a brace, and thus convert it into a very powerful screwdriver. The double-ended pattern is particularly useful.

What is a bradawl used for?

The main use is for making the pilot holes needed when inserting screws. Different sizes of blade are available, which can be readily sharpened with a fine file. In use, the cutting edge is placed across the grain so that the fibres are severed as pressure is applied.

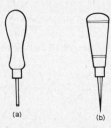

Fig. 19. The two popular types of bradawl: (a) standard, and (b) birdcage

An alternative shape for a bradawl is where the blade is of tapering square section, useful because large and small holes can be made with it. This is known as the birdcage pattern, and both types are shown in Fig. 19. An alternative name for bradawls is sprigbits.

What are the differences between back saws and hand saws?

Back saws are those which have their blades stiffened with a strip of either steel or brass along the back edge. Saws in this group include the tenon saw with a typical length of 254 mm (10 in) and 15 points per 25 mm (1 in), dovetail saw with a length of 203 mm (8 in) and up to 20 points per 25 mm, and gent's saw with a length of 152 mm (6 in), and again up to 20 points per 25 mm.

Tenon saws are used for general bench work including cross-cutting small stock and forming most joints. The dovetail saw is used particularly for cutting dovetail joints and where accuracy is extremely important, while the gent's saw is for very light work and model making.

The three common variations of handsaw are the rip, cross cut, and panel. Handsaws have flexible blades, the back edge of which may be straight ('straight' backs), or curved ('skew' backs). Better-quality ones are 'taper' ground, which means the blade is thinner at the back than at the teeth. This helps to provide clearance of the blade within the cut, and makes for improved sawing.

The rip saw is tending to go out of favour, partly because of the increasing availability of PAR timber, and also because of the growing popularity of small circular saws. This saw has teeth shaped and sharpened for cutting along the grain, also known as ripping.

Cross cut saws have a length of around 560 mm–610 mm (22 in–24 in), and usually with 7 points per 25 mm. Their teeth are designed for cutting across the grain of wood, but they will cut along the grain although with a little less efficiency. Generally used on thicker wood, say over 25 mm (1 in).

The panel saw is really a smaller version of the cross cut, with lengths between 457 mm–560 mm (18 in–22 in), and invariably with 10 points per 25 mm. This is an ideal saw for cutting material up to around 25 mm (1 in) thick, and is also the saw to use for sheet material such as plywood, chipboard, and blockboard. When cutting these boards, it is essential to use a saw with fairly fine teeth, or splitting on the underside will occur.

What is meant by the terms 'set', and 'points per 25 mm' when related to saws?

Set is the bending of alternate teeth to the left or right, its purpose being to ensure the cut, or kerf, made by the blade is slightly wider than the thickness of the blade. The amount of set is proportional to the size of the teeth. If too little set is given, the saw will 'bind' in the kerf; if too great then both wood and energy are being wasted, and the sawing is harder to control. Fig. 20 shows the end view of the teeth of a saw of cross-cut type where the set is shown exaggerated. In practice, only approximately the top third of the teeth is bent outwards, this usually with a plier-like tool called a saw set.

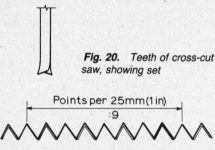

Fig. 20. Teeth of cross-cut saw, showing set

Fig. 21. Determining saw teeth size

Points per 25 mm (1 in) is the term still used to determine the size of the teeth, as shown in Fig. 21. Note that the points at both ends of the measurement are included. In this diagram, 9 points per 25 mm means 8 actual teeth.

What saws are used for cutting curves?

Saws for cutting curves must have narrow blades to enable them to negotiate the restrictions of a kerf which is not straight. Because narrow blades are weak, the saws often incorporate a frame so that the blade can be put into tension.

The most used of the frame saws is probably the coping, with a blade of around 152 mm (6 in) in length. It is shown in Fig. 22; it has a frame of spring steel tensioned by tightening the handle. The blade can be inserted with the teeth pointing either 'forward' or 'backward' – depending on which way suits a particular user. The blade can be rotated within the frame. Used for wood up to around 19 mm (¾ in) thick.

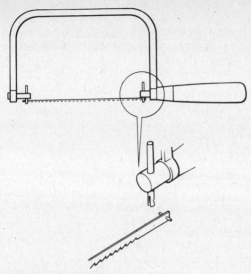

Fig. 22. Coping saw

The bow saw is a larger version of the coping, although it looks rather different with its wooden frame and its tensioning arrangement by twisted string. It is used for cutting thicker material.

The fret saw is also metal-framed. The blades are 127 mm (5 in) in length, very fine with up to 32 points per 25 mm. It is used only on very thin wood, but can produce extremely intricate shapes.

All the above saws are restricted by their frames, and cannot operate at a greater distance from the edge of the wood than that imposed by the frame.

The key-hole saw, also known as the padsaw, has a fairly narrow blade held directly in a handle, but no frame. While the saw can therefore be used well away from the edges of the wood, the unsupported blade is easily buckled. The compass saw is a larger version of the key-hole, but its relatively wide blade – up to 19 mm (¾ in) – makes it suitable only for very gentle curves.

Is a claw hammer more useful than a Warrington pattern?

This depends very much on the type of work carried out. The average claw hammer is about twice the weight of a Warrington hammer, and is therefore intended for driving in medium and large nails. The claw hammer is much used on constructional work, its claw making the removal of nails fairly easy.

The Warrington pattern, with popular weights of 8 oz or 10 oz, is only suitable for driving in smaller nails, and because of this is regarded more of a bench tool. A pin hammer is a lightweight version of the Warrington, its 4 oz head making it ideal for fine nails and panel pins.

How is the size of a screwdriver determined?

Screwdrivers for the traditional slot-headed screws are measured by the length of the blade, with the width of the tip in proportion to this. There are, though, exceptions to this where the blade is 'extra long', and also with a very short model known as 'stubby'.

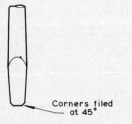

Corners filed at 45°

***Fig. 23.** Tip of screwdriver after grinding off corners*

When using a screwdriver, one should be selected which just fits the slot of the screw. If too large, it is likely to damage the wood, if too small it will be difficult to use. Some users like to grind the corners away as in Fig. 23, so as to match the countersinking of a screw head and thus obtain a better fit in the slot.

Cross-head screws are now invariably of the 'Supadriv' type, and must have a screwdriver blade to match. With these drivers, the tip of the blade is the critical part, and are available in four sizes. The size required depends on the gauge of the screw being inserted, as follows:

Blade number 1 for screw gauges 3 and 4
Blade number 2 for screw gauges 5 – 10
Blade number 3 for screw gauges 11 – 12
Blade number 4 for screw gauges over 12

Screwdrivers are also known as turnscrews.

What is meant by 'sharpening angles'?

For most 'edge' tools, there are two angles of sharpening: the grinding angle and the honing angle, and these are shown in Fig. 24. The purpose of grinding is to quickly remove excess metal from behind the cutting edge, and thus reduce the amount of metal presented to the oilstone during honing. Grinding is also used to restore a blade which has been damaged.

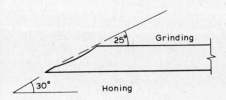

Fig. 24. *Grinding and honing angles for edge tools*

The honing angle is that presented to the oilstone, and produces the actual cutting edge. Because of the thinness of most plane blades, the need for grinding is diminished, and therefore such blades are very often sharpened with a single honing angle only.

While there is some tolerance in the angles shown, if too steep the cutting efficiency is reduced, if too flat the tip of the blade will be weak.

33

What is a suitable oilstone for general use?

For serious work, the size of the stone should be
152 mm × 50 mm × 25 mm (6 in × 2 in × 1 in), and preferably
203 mm (8 in) long. For most purposes, a medium-grit artificial
stone will give perfectly satisfactory results. However, double-
sided stones are prefered by some, with combinations of either
fine and medium, or medium and coarse. Natural stones are very
expensive, and to some extent have gone out of favour because of
the improvement in man-made stones. A special box should be
made for an oilstone, complete with lid.

What are the essential stages of sharpening an edge tool?

The stages are as follows:

(a) Place a small amount of oil on the stone. This should be a light
oil, never a drying oil such as linseed.

(b) Place the blade on the stone at a fairly low angle, and lift
slowly until the tip of the blade is seen to be in contact with the
stone.

(c) Rub to and fro with a fair amount of pressure. The wrists must
be 'locked' for this, to ensure that the blade remains at a constant

Fig. 25. *When sharpening a blade, keep its angle constant*

angle (see Fig. 25). Rocking of the blade results in a rounded bevel
which is unsatisfactory. As far as possible, the whole surface of
the stone should be used.

(d) Continue rubbing until a 'burr' can be detected on the upper
surface. This can readily be felt by drawing a finger off the blade
where the rubbing has taken place.

34

(e) Remove the burr by rubbing the back of the blade on the oilstone. This must be done with the blade absolutely flat and in complete contact with the stone. Never attempt to form a bevel on the reverse side.

(f) Repeat stages (d) and (e), using light pressure and making only a few strokes.

(g) Often the burr will become completely detached in the form of a fine sliver of steel, known as the 'wire edge'.

(h) To remove the burr if it does not become detached, and in any case to improve the edge, stropping is the last stage. A strop is a piece of leather glued to a piece of wood. This has an overall length of around 280 mm (11 in), and is shown in Fig. 26. The

Fig. 26. Leather strop

blade is drawn backwards on its bevel on the leather, then this is repeated on the reverse side with the blade flat. Several strokes are made, the leather being periodically treated with buffing compound, crocus powder, or very fine emery powder.

Power tools

How is the size of a power drill determined?

In two ways:

1. The capacity of the chuck. Most drills now have chucks of either 10 mm (3/8 in), or 13 mm (1/2 in). This partly determines the size of drill which can be accommodated, and bears some relationship to the power of the motor.

35

2. The power of the motor is the second way in which drill size is rated. The power of the motor, or its electrical size, is measured in watts. The higher the wattage rating, the greater the power of the drill.

Although not directly related to the size of the drill, other factors which affect its performance include:

● Speed. Many drills, especially the better-quality ones, have two speeds: high for wood, and slow for metals and other hard materials.
● Variable-speed option. The speed is infinitely variable to its upper limit, and is adjusted by pressure on the trigger.
● Hammer-action option. This facility can be 'switched on' to increase the efficiency when drilling masonry and allied materials.

What types of bit can be used in a power drill?

For small holes in wood, engineers' morse drills are ideal, and can be obtained in a very wide range of sizes. Countersinks for metal also work well in wood. Although most 'machine' wood bits can be used in a power drill, the flat bit has been developed specially

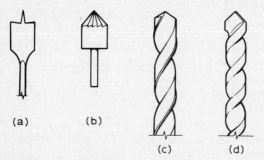

(a)   (b)   (c)   (d)

Fig. 27. Bits and drills for use in power drill: (a) flat bit, (b) countersink for wood and metal, (c) engineer's morse drill, and (d) tipped masonry drill

for this purpose. The fairly large point is needed to locate and guide the drill, and these bits are remarkably efficient even though they operate by scraping rather than actual cutting. They will bore in all directions of the grain, including holes made at an angle. They are easily sharpened by file.

For brickwork, concrete and masonry, tungsten-carbide tipped (TCT) drills are essential; these are known as masonry drills. They cannot be sharpened with standard facilities, but instead need to be ground on what is known as a 'green grit' wheel.

A selection of bits is shown in Fig. 27.

What is a power-drill rebating attachment?

A rebating attachment is a small circular saw, usually about 51 mm (2 in) diameter, the spindle of which fits directly into the chuck. The body of the attachment includes a sole plate, and a fence, both of which are adjustable. When cutting rebates, two

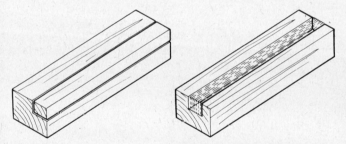

Fig. 28. Rebate formed by two saw cuts

Fig. 29. Groove formed by a series of 'passes'

cuts are made from adjacent surfaces to remove a strip of wood, as shown in Fig. 28.

The attachment can also be used to form grooves. For this operation, a series of cuts, or 'passes' as they are known, are made, as seen in Fig. 29.

The attachment is particularly useful in chipboard, as forming both rebates and grooves in this material is not satisfactory by traditional hand methods.

What are the differences between a disc sander, an orbital sander and a belt sander?

Disc sanders may be fixed or portable. With the fixed type, the abrasive paper is fixed to a rigid flat plate, and a table is provided for supporting the work. They are used mostly for trimming and shaping purposes, rather than final smoothing.

Portable disc sanders invariably take the form of drill attachments, and are usually about 127 mm (5 in) in diameter. The abrasive paper is normally mounted on a rubber backing to provide flexibility. These sanders are usually used for smoothing work which is to be painted, and often for improving surfaces which have already been painted before repainting. These sanders are not suitable for surfaces which are to receive a clear finish, as their rotary action leaves circular score marks. Indeed, great care is needed when using a disc sander, or pronounced circular grooves can be quickly created.

Orbital sanders work in an oscillating movement, and are often called finishing sanders. This name describes them well, as they are only suitable for fine sanding of surfaces which are already level and in reasonable condition.

Belt sanders have an endless belt of abrasive fabric, revolving around two drums with a pressure plate between. The belts vary from 63 mm–102 mm (2½ in–4 in). These are highly efficient machines, capable of removing a fair amount of wood quite quickly, and because of this usually have dust bags fitted.

Why are routers becoming so popular?

High-speed routers are popular because their versatility is being realised more and more. They are capable of grooving and trenching, chamfering and bevelling, moulding, and many allied operations. Furthermore, they can carry these out on both straight and curved work. The range of cutters is constantly being increased, many are TCT, and refinements such as 'plunge action', templates and guides add to the usefulness of the tool. By using the machine inverted in a router table, the router can then be used as a small spindle.

What type of sawing are jig saws intended for?

Jig saws are primarily intended for sawing curves and intricate shapes which cannot be sawn with either a handsaw, or a back saw. Like the equivalent hand tools for sawing curves, the jig saw has a narrow blade which allows it to negotiate cuts which are not straight. Jig saws will of course make straight cuts as well, and most models have an adjustable sole enabling bevel cuts to be made. For internal cut-outs, a hole has to be made to allow the blade to start its cut. A variation of the jig saw is a scroll saw, where the blade can be made to rotate within the body, thus allowing greater manoeuvrability.

Blades can be fitted to jig saws, enabling them to cut a wide variety of materials other than wood.

Can bandsaws tackle all kinds of curved work?

No; bandsaws have a number of limiting factors. The first is known as the throat size, which is the distance from the blade to the frame which supports the upper part of the machine. This dimension limits the distance at which the blade can operate from the edge of the wood.

There is also the size of the smallest radius that can be sawn. This depends very largely on the width of the blade, 6 mm (1/4 in) being the narrowest usually available. While narrow blades can tackle fairly small curves as well as flatter ones, they are weaker and more prone to breaking.

Bandsaws cannot make cuts which are completely internal.

There is also the thickness of the wood which can be sawn. Even small machines can cut wood which is 51 mm (2 in) thick and even more, and bandsaws are designed so that the maximum thickness of wood which can be sawn is related to the general robustness of the machine, and the power of its motor.

What operations other than straight sawing can be performed on a circular saw?

To a large extent it depends on the refinements on the saw, such as:

(a) Can the amount of blade projecting above the table be adjusted? This is said to be a blade with 'rise and fall' provision, although on some small saw benches it is the table which actually moves.

(b) Can the blade (or table) be made to 'cant', or tilt, so that the angle between the two is other than 90°?

(c) Does the machine have provision for 'wobble' sawing, an arrangement whereby the blade oscilates as it rotates, thus making a kerf much wider than the thickness of the teeth?

A large proportion of even small saws (say with a blade diameter of 200 mm (8 in)) do have the above provisions, as well as a cross-cut slide. The following are among the operations which can be carried out on such a saw:

Ripping; cross cutting; bevel sawing; mitre and angle cutting; combined angle-bevel cutting; rebating; grooving (even without the wobble saw); trenching and angle trenching; taper sawing (with simple home-made jig); and tenoning.

It is also possible to carry out box combing on a circular saw, but a special jig is needed for this.

Equipment

What is the difference between a 'plain' vice and a 'quick-release' vice?

With a plain vice, the movement of the outer jaw is controlled directly and only by rotation of the handle which is fitted to the main thread. A quick-release vice has a small lever at the front, which when depressed disengages the main thread from the body of the vice, enabling the outer jaw to be simply and quickly slid in and out; actual tightening of the jaw on the workpiece is carried out by releasing the lever and turning the handle. A plain vice has a 'square' thread, and a quick-release vice has a thread known as a 'buttress'.

How is a vice fixed to the bench, and why are wooden facings added to the vice jaws?

There are two methods of securing a vice to a bench: by using coach screws, or coach bolts. A coach screw is a very heavy-duty screw requiring a spanner to insert it. It has a square head for this purpose. A coach bolt is a bolt specially designed for use with wood, having a domed head with a square shank immediately below the head to prevent rotation in the wood. A coach bolt is usually fitted with a square nut.

Coach screws can be used for securing smallish vices, say up to 150 mm (6 in) jaws. Larger vices, which extend much further, are best fixed with coach bolts. Because these are arranged to pass right through the bench top, they offer a very positive anchorage. The heads of the bolts should be recessed into the bench top, then the holes filled to ensure that the tools cannot make contact with them. Vices are usually secured so that the top edge of the jaws are about 50 mm (½ in) lower than the top of the bench, so that these too can be protected.

The main purpose of the wooden facings is to protect the workpiece from being bruised by the vice's metal jaws, and also to prevent tools from being damaged by the jaws which are usually made of cast iron.

Can a sash cramp be extended?

Lengthening bars are available for sash cramps, although to ensure that they function properly they must be bought to 'match' the cramps being extended. The bars have a length of 915 mm (36 in) or thereabouts.

Cramps can also be extended by bolting two together. The sliding shoes, and the retaining screws at the end of the sash, must be removed, then a couple of nuts and bolts used to secure them together.

What are cramp heads?

Cramp heads are the parts of a cramp between which the workpiece is actually gripped. Cramp heads enable an economical sash cramp to be made at home, and to any reasonable length. A piece of timber 25 mm (1 in) thick and about 63 mm (2½ in) wide is used to make the bar, with a series of holes bored along its length into which the pins in the heads locate and provide for adjustment.

What advantage does a bench holdfast have over a G-cramp?

A bench holdfast can be used at any position on the bench top, providing that holes are bored in the bench, and 'collars' fitted in the holes. The G-cramp's frame limits the extent to which it can operate from the edge. In addition, the bench top must have an overhang to enable the shoe of the cramp to grip.

What is an edging cramp?

An edging cramp is similar to a G-cramp, but with a second screw positioned half way round the body, so that this operates at right angles to the main screw. It is used to exert pressure onto the edge of the workpiece, as for instance when lipping is being secured.

Why is it important to place scrap wood between the cramp and the workpiece?

Cramps exert considerable pressure, and because of the fairly small area of the shoe part of the cramp which transmits this pressure, and the cramp itself usually being metal, bruising of the wood can easily take place. Protecting the work from possible damage from cramps is particularly important when the wood has already been well smoothed and is ready for applying a finish.

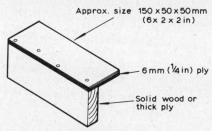

Approx. size 150 x 50 x 50 mm
(6 x 2 x 2 in)

6 mm (¼ in) ply

Solid wood or thick ply

Fig. 30.   *Cramping block*

The scrap protects the workpiece in two ways: (a) the pressure from the cramp is spread over a wide area providing it is reasonably large; (b) the scrap, being far less hard than the cramp, is not likely to bruise the workpiece. For sash cramps, it is worth-while making a number of the cramping blocks as shown in Fig. 30.

What is the purpose of a sawing board?

A sawing board is an important piece of equipment, and is in regular use in all areas of woodworking. The board has two purposes: (a) it protects the bench from the inevitable damage from the saw as a cut is completed; (b) it provides a simple but most effective way of holding the wood quite firmly while being cut.

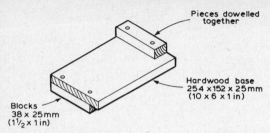

Fig. 31. Sawing board

Sawing boards are used particularly with tenon saws when sawing wood of fairly small section. They can be bought or home-made; details are given in Fig. 31. They can be made right-, left-, or dual-handed.

What is a shooting board?

This is shown in Fig. 32; it enables the end of a piece of wood to be planed without the corners being split. Because of the

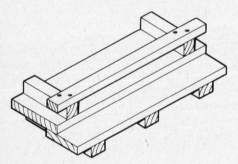

Fig. 32. Reversible-pattern shooting board

considerable risk of splitting when end grain is planed, special precautions have to be taken, of which the use of the shooting board is one technique. Planing end grain is known as 'shooting', and shooting boards can also be bought or home-made.

What is the difference between a mitre box and a mitre block?

Mitre boxes and blocks are very similar pieces of equipment, used for the repetition cutting of mitres with (usually) a back saw. The mitre box is for fairly large work, while the block is for small work such as glazing beads and mouldings. With both mitre

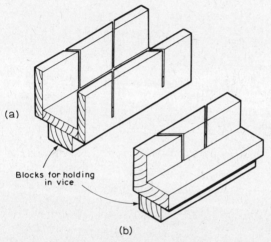

(a)

Blocks for holding in vice

(b)

Fig. 33. *(a) Mitre box, and (b) mitre block*

boxes and blocks, angles other than 45° can be cut, providing saw cuts are first made to the angle required. Fig. 33 shows these pieces of equipment, which are best made of a hardwood such as beech. Blocks of wood screwed to the underside enable easy gripping in the vice.

Can a cramp be used when assembling a picture frame?

Various cramps are available for use when assembling picture frames, and other mitred corners. The commonest cramp is

45

known as a corner cramp; this caters for a single mitre only and holds the two pieces securely together to exactly 90°. The wood can be glued and nailed while so held.

A more sophisticated cramp enables the four pieces of a frame to be simultaneously glued and assembled. The single tightening screw allows for equal pressure to be applied to all corners, thus ensuring the frame is square.

A very simple framing cramp consists of four corner blocks of plastic, and a strong cord which connects the blocks together and which can be readily tightened. The blocks exert pressure on the mitres, and hold the frame together while gluing. Only limited pressure can be exerted, but this simple cramp does have other uses, for instance when re-gluing the loosened parts of a dining chair.

What is a squaring lath?

This is a strip of wood, say around 13 mm × 13 mm (½ in × ½ in), with one end pointed. It is used to measure the diagonals of a frame type of construction when it is being assembled. In use, a pencil mark is made on the lath when the first diagonal is measured with it, then the other diagonal checked to see if it is the same. If needs be, the cramps are adjusted until equal diagonals are attained. A squaring lath is much more

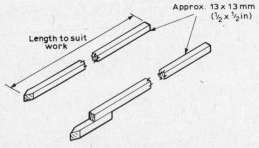

Fig. 34. *Two variations of a squaring lath*

46

accurate on large work than a try square used in the corners, and its use is based on the fact that the diagonals on a square and a rectangle are equal. Fig. 34 shows two variations on a squaring lath.

What are winding sticks used for?

They are used to test the flatness of a fairly wide board. They are used in pairs, each one being positioned near the end of the board

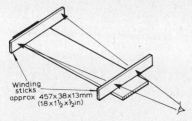

Winding sticks approx 457x38x13mm (18 x 1½ x ½in)

Fig. 35. *Use of winding sticks*

as shown in Fig. 35. By sighting across the top edges of the sticks, any 'twist' in the board is soon detected. Winding sticks must be accurately made out of sound, dry wood, and are usually about 457 mm × 38 mm × 13 mm (18 in × 1½ in × ½ in).

3
Preparing timber and marking-out

What are the main stages of preparing a piece of rough wood to a specific size, by hand?

The procedure is as follows:
1. The better side is selected. It is then planed smooth by removing the minimum amount of wood, and tested with a straight edge lengthways, crossways, and cornerways. Further shavings are removed until the surface is true.
2. The face edge – the better edge – is prepared next, and tested along its length with a straight edge, and crossways with a try square to check the angle. The try square must be held tightly against the face side, as this is the angle being checked.
3. The wood is now gauged to the width required. The gauge is set to this width, held against and moved along the face edge so as to scribe a line along the face of the wood, and repeated on the opposite side. The excess wood is planed off, with constant testing as at (2).
4. The wood is gauged to the required thickness, with the gauge being held against the face side so as to scribe a line along both edges, and both ends. The waste is planed off, and again the surface frequently checked by eye, by measuring the thickness, and by using a straight edge on the surface.

These stages are shown in Fig. 36.

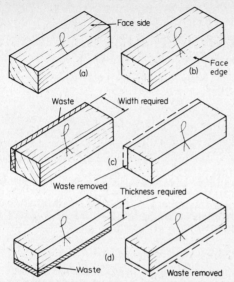

Fig. 36. *Preparing wood to size: (a) marking the face side, (b) marking the face edge, (c) gauging and planing to the required width, and (d) gauging and planing to the required thickness*

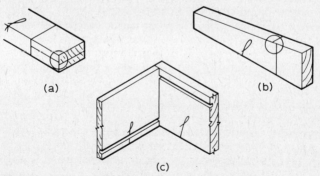

Fig. 37. *Importance of following face marks (see text)*

Why are face marks so important?

The face side and face edge of the wood act as datum surfaces, against which the stocks of gauges, squares and other marking-out tools should normally abut in use. The face and edge marks are also used to indicate which part of the wood is the 'inside', the 'front', and the 'top'. Examples of common errors when face marks are ignored are shown in Fig. 37(a) where the gauge has been reversed during gauging the end; (b), when 'squaring round', the try square has not at each step been held against the face marks, hence the lines do not meet on all corners.

Face marks are also used to indicate where certain cuts are to be made, such as grooves, rebates and trenches. Fig. 37(c) shows the inside corner of a drawer, where the groove on the front has been wrongly made because the face marks have been ignored.

What plane is best for preparing timber to size?

When truing-up timber of average length, and for quick removal of excess material, the jack plane is the most suitable to use. Being longer than a smoothing plane, it will give more accurate results than smaller alternatives.

For extreme accuracy, and for very large work, a trying plane is to be preferred, as this is considerably longer than a jack plane.

When timber is being prepared, what allowances should be made on its sizes?

If the timber has first to be sawn, an allowance of approximately 1.5 mm (¹⁄₁₆ in) should be made on each surface for the planing. No allowance is then made at the planing stage, the width and thickness being planed to the net sizes. However, extra should be allowed on the length, about 19 mm–25 mm (¾ in–1 in) being usual. This is to allow for precise squaring-up of the ends if needed, for 'joggles' to be left at the ends of morticed members, and for such things as protruding tenons to be subsequently levelled off.

What are the basic stages for marking-out a simple frame with half-lap joints?

Place two members of the frame in the vice. Using a try square, mark off a small amount of waste at one end, and from this line measure the overall length required. Note that the first stage in marking-out is normally to indicate the length, with the waste clearly marked. This is shown in Fig. 38(a). From these lines, measure distances equal to the width of the material, as these

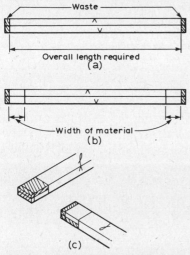

Fig. 38. *Marking-out for half-lap joints (see text)*

indicate the extent of the joints (Fig. 38*b*). These distances can be established, or at least checked, by using the wood itself as the means of measuring. Now remove the pieces from the vice, and square round the lines individually.

Set a marking gauge to exactly half the thickness of the wood, and gauge the joints by having the stock of the gauge against the face side.

The two remaining parts of the frame should be marked-out in exactly the same way, to indicate the overall width required, and are also gauged from the face side. Note, though, that the waste on these two members is on the opposite side to the first pair, so that the face side will be the same way round on assembly. Fig. 38(c) shows the final stage.

If the frame is square rather than rectangular, then all four pieces can be initially marked-out while held together. It is standard practice to mark-out similar parts all together, as far as this is possible.

Is there any difference between 'setting-out' and 'marking-out'?

These terms are very similar, but there is a difference. Setting out is where full-size drawings are made of a project, although such drawings often only need to show certain parts of the work. They

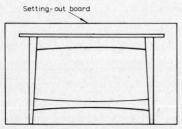

Setting-out board

Fig. 39. *Setting-out for small table*

may be made of paper, plywood, hardboard, or solid wood, and are particularly important if the work is curved, shaped, splayed or tapered, or wherever it involves angles other than 90°, and components which are not parallel. Fig. 39 shows a simple example of setting-out, this being the side view of a table which involves tapers, bevelled tenons, and curved members. For frame constructions like doors and windows, the setting-out is often carried out on a strip of wood, and known as a setting-out rod.

52

Marking-out is where the marking-out tools are used on the actual wood. On more complicated work, information for the marking-out is often transferred directly from the setting-out.

How is a sliding bevel set to a particular angle?

There are two ways in which angles are expressed, (a) by degrees, and (b) by ratio. In both cases, the usual method is first to establish the angle on a piece of plywood. Where the angle is expressed in degrees, a protractor is used to mark out the angle required, as the example shown in Fig. 40(a). The sliding bevel is then set to the line marked on the wood.

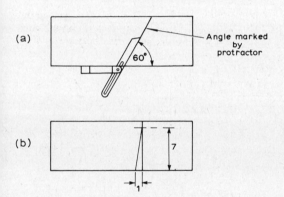

Fig. 40. Setting a sliding bevel (see text)

Where the angle or slope is expressed as a ratio, for example 1:7, a line is first squared across the wood. Along this line is marked-off a distance of seven units of measurement, and from the base of the line is marked one unit of measurement along the edge of the wood. Joining up the two points gives the required slope, to which the sliding bevel can be set (Fig. 40*b*). Angles for dovetails are usually indicated as ratios.

53

'Units of measurement' can be of any convenient size, and will not alter the angle providing the same unit is used for both distances required.

What are 'identical' and 'handed' components?

The term identical means components which are exactly the same as one another in every sense, and which are therefore interchangeable. Handed components are where the parts are made as a 'pair', that is, one right-handed and one left-handed.

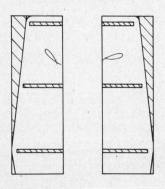

Fig. 41. 'Handed' ends of shelving unit

Fig. 41 shows the ends of a simple shelving unit, with shaped outline and trenches to hold the shelves, and is an example of where the two pieces must be made 'handed'.

If a component has to be tapered, when should this be done?

This depends on the size of the part, the amount of taper, and whether the taper is effectively on one edge, or both. Generally, parts which are to be tapered should not be so shaped until after the joints have been cut. Fig. 42(a) shows the end of a small table where the upright is tapered on both edges. If these tapers were formed at the preparation stage, marking-out the top and bottom of the piece would present problems, as clearly a try square could not be used. By marking-out and cutting the ends of this piece before the tapering takes place, the work becomes straightforward.

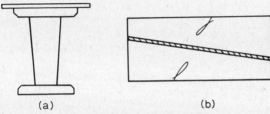

Fig. 42. *Tapered components: (a) table with tapered legs, (b) marking-out 'side-by-side'*

Sometimes it is far more economical to cut two pieces which are tapered 'side-by-side', as shown in Fig. 41(b). Where the taper is on one edge, it is usual to make the opposite edge into the face edge. This is important insofar as marking out is then made at right angles, and parallel, to this edge. If two pieces are being cut as shown in Fig. 42(b), and the material is, for example, a man-made board with a special facing on one side only, then the two pieces so produced will be 'identical' rather than a 'pair'.

How are curves best marked out?

Assuming the curve is an arc, that is a part of a circle, it depends very much on the size, or radius. Small curves, such as the rounded corners of an occasional table, can be marked with compasses, or more simply pencilling round a circular tin of convenient size. For a large curve, a makeshift but efficient 'beam' compass can be made from a strip of wood around 16 mm × 6 mm (⅞ in × ¼ in), with one end notched to take a pencil, and a nail driven through the lath at the appropriate distance on which the compass can rotate. This is shown in Fig. 43(a).

A 'flat' curve is one where the radius is very large, and where using a beam compass is not a practical method. The usual procedure here is to mark the ends of the curve, and its mid-point

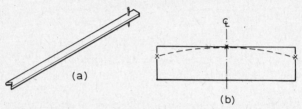

Fig. 43. *Marking-out for curves*

as shown in Fig. 43(b). A thin lath is then bent to line up with the three points, and the curve marked by drawing along the lath, usually with the help of an assistant.

When are templates used in woodwork?

Templates are used where the shape of the component is fairly complex, and where by making the template the marking-out and subsequent stages are made easier, and the results better. They become more important where multiple components are required to the same outline. A template for a curved leg is shown in Fig. 44(a), which also indicates the tenons at the ends, and the shoulder lines. Templates can be made from plywood, hardboard, solid wood, or even cardboard.

Often it is an advantage to make only a 'half' template. Fig. 44(b) shows the top member of a Welsh dresser, and (c) illustrates the half template of the decorative edge. By reversing the template on the centre line, uniformity of the two halves is assured.

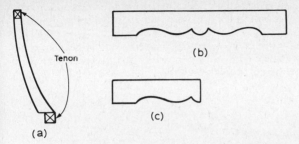

Fig. 44. (a) Template for curved leg, (b) top member of Welsh dresser, and (c) template for (b)

Templates can also be used to actually guide an electric router when the router is being used to cut out a profile of compound shape. The router must be fitted with an attachment to allow this work to be carried out.

What is a dovetail template?

This can take various forms, but essentially it is a device to enable the slope required for dovetails to be marked out simply and uniformly. Two are shown in Fig. 45: (a) is made from wood, and is always home-produced, while (b) is metal and may be bought or home-made. The actual angle, or slope, is of course fixed.

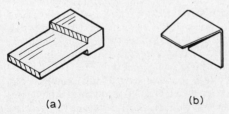

Fig. 45. Dovetail templates: (a) is wood, (b) is metal

How are simple geometrical shapes like hexagons and octagons marked out?

Both hexagons and octagons occur fairly frequently in wood-work, the hexagon being a figure of six sides with an internal angle of 120°, and an octagon of eight sides with an internal angle of 135°.

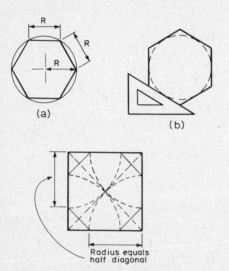

Fig. 46. *(a) Hexagon constructed using compasses, (b) hexagon constructed using set square, and (c) octagon constructed within a square*

A circle which encloses a hexagon is known as the circumscribing circle, whose diameter must equal the distance across the corners of the hexagon. If this circle is drawn, the radius of the circle will step off around the circumference exactly six times, thus giving the six corners of the hexagon. This always applies, regardless of size, and is shown in Fig. 46(a).

If the information given is the distance across the sides, rather than the corners, then a circle of this size is first drawn. The hexagon is then constructed on the outside of the circle, using a 60°–30° set square, which gives the six sides, as shown in Fig. 46(b).

For an octagon, first draw a square equal to the size of the octagon required. Draw in the diagonals, then step-off distances from each corner equal to half a diagonal, to give two points on each side of the square. Joining up the eight points produced gives a regular octagon, and is illustrated in Fig. 46(c).

4
Joints

What is a stopped mortice and tenon?

This is where the mortice is cut into the wood on one surface only, without penetrating all the way through. The joint, therefore, is concealed on completion. It is also known as a 'blind' mortice.

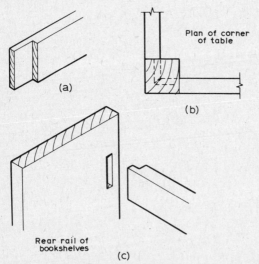

(a)

Plan of corner of table

(b)

Rear rail of bookshelves

(c)

Fig. 47. *Bare-faced tenons (see text)*

What is a bare-faced tenon, and when is it used?

A bare-faced tenon is a tenon which has only one shoulder, as shown in Fig. 47(a). The application is where the joint is being used near the edge of the work, where cutting the mortice too close to the edge would cause a weakness. By using a bare-faced tenon, the joint is kept as far away from the edge as is practicable, while retaining alignment of outer surfaces. Fig. 47(b) shows bare-faced tenons as applied to the legs of a table, where it is desired to keep the outer surfaces flush. Note that it is usual practice to mitre the ends of tenons which meet at right angles within a morticed member. The tenons may also be of the haunched type. Fig. 47(c) illustrates the bare-faced tenon as might be used on a shelving unit between the ends and a top rail.

What is a haunched tenon?

This is a tenon whose width is reduced to make a more satisfactory joint at the corner of a framing. By adjusting the

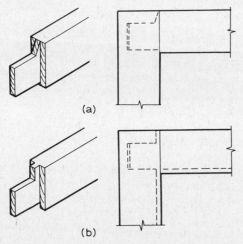

(a)

(b)

Fig. 48. *(a) Sloping and (b) square haunches*

61

width of the tenon in this way, the mortice need not be cut right up to the end of the wood, and therefore loss of strength is minimised. The actual haunch provides some location within the morticed member, and helps to lessen the risk of distortion.

Haunches may be sloping, as at Fig. 48(a), or square, as at (b). The sloping haunch is neater insofar as it is concealed, but the square haunch has to be adopted if the inner edges of the frame is grooved, as it would be for panelled-type work.

With haunched tenons, it is usual to reduce the width of the wood by approximately one third. Haunched joints may be stopped or through, barefaced, or of other variations.

What is the difference between double and twin tenons?

These terms are very similar, and are often confused even in woodworking textbooks. Double tenons are shown in Fig. 49(a),

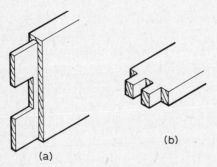

Fig. 49. Tenons: (a) double and (b) twin

where in effect the two tenons have been formed from one larger one. They are used where the length of a single mortice would be so great as to create a weakness. Note the 'haunch' between the tenons. Double tenons are much used on joinery work, especially on doors of traditional type.

Twin tenons are cut side by side, rather than end-on, as seen at Fig. 49(b). This joint is used more in furniture making, for example at the ends of drawer rails.

What is the usual proportion for the thickness of the tenon in a mortice and tenon joint?

The normal proportion for the tenon where the pieces of wood being jointed are of equal thickness is to make the tenon one third of this thickness, or slightly more to the nearest convenient dimension. For example, in wood 22 mm (7/8 in) thick, the tenon would be made 8 mm (5/16 in).

Where the pieces being jointed are such that the thickness of the component to be morticed is greater than the member being tenoned, it is preferable to increase the proportion of the tenon up to around half that of the wood on which this part of the joint is being made.

What are the various types of half-lap joint?

Half-lap joints are usually used for simple frame constructions. Variations of the joint are shown in Fig. 50. While the joints are

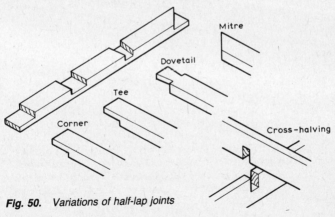

Fig. 50. *Variations of half-lap joints*

usually made by cutting away half the thickness of the wood, they can be formed on the edge of the material by cutting away half the width. The cross-halving joint in particular is often cut this way as shown.

Can 'halving' joints be made less than half the thickness of the wood?

While the term half-lap joint implies that half the wood is cut away on each piece, resulting in the surfaces of both parts being flush on assembly, the principle of the half-lap joint can be varied

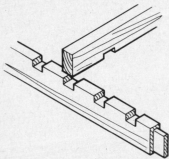

Fig. 51. Adaptation of cross-halving

whereby less than half the wood is cut away. An example is shown in Fig. 51, which shows the cross rail at the end of a small table, and one of a series of slats which would form a lower shelf to the table.

What slope should be used for dovetails?

The traditionally accepted slope for dovetails is 1:6 for softwoods, and 1:8 for hardwoods. The increased slope for softwoods is because these timbers will compress more on assembly. In practice, many craftsmen use a slope of 1:7 for all timbers.

What is a lap dovetail, and where is it used?

This is shown in Fig. 52, where the wood on one component is arranged to 'lap' the joint so as to conceal it on one side. It is used

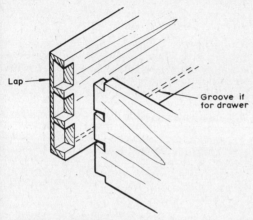

Lap

Groove if
for drawer

Fig. 52. Lap dovetail joint

where the joint needs to be hidden on one surface and not the other, and is the standard joint for drawer fronts, where the thickness of the front is usually greater than the sides.

What are the basic types of housing joint?

A housing joint is formed where one member is trenched, with the second component fitting into it. The three basic types of housing are shown in Fig. 53 – (a) is the 'through' housing, (b) is a 'stopped' joint which is concealed at one edge, and (c) is a 'double-stopped' housing. Housing joints are particularly used where the wood is fairly wide, for example on bookshelves.

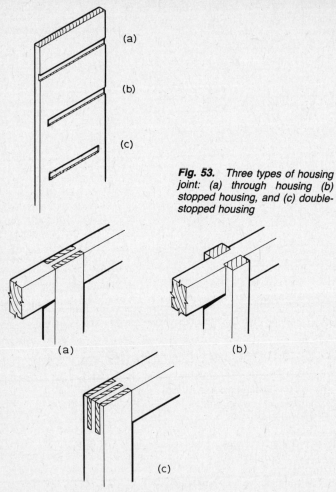

Fig. 53. Three types of housing joint: (a) through housing (b) stopped housing, and (c) double-stopped housing

Fig. 54. Bridle joint variations (see text)

Other variations of the joint include the dovetail housing, and one which also incorporates mortice and tenons. With all housing joints, it is usual to make the depth of the trench around one third the thickness of the wood.

When is a bridle joint adopted?

A bridle joint has similarities to a mortice and tenon, but with the 'opposite' parts cut away as waste. It is shown in its simplest form in Fig. 54(a). This joint is particularly suitable where a wider piece of wood is being jointed into a thinner one, as shown at (b), and is often adopted as the joint between the legs and rails of items of furniture. A variation of this joint is where the trench is cut on one side only.

Bridle joints can also be used at the corner of a frame, and may be of single or multiple form as shown at (c). This joint is now widely used on the construction of window sashes, although it has to be modified to allow for rebates and moulded edges.

What joints can be used for 'box' constructions?

As well as different types of dovetail joint which can be used, three fairly common 'box' joints are shown in Fig. 55. While the rebated joint at (a) has little mechanical strength, it is easy to cut, and has the advantage that it can be pinned in both directions. Pins driven in in this way have a locking effect which results in considerable strength.

The joint at (b) is a comb or finger joint. As well as the interlocking effect created, the area of wood of each piece is considerably increased, and thus the effectiveness of gluing the joint is improved a great deal.

The tongued corner joint is shown at (c). It is important not to make the tongue too thick, or the wood between the groove and

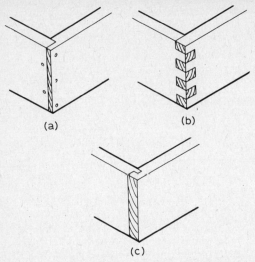

Fig. 55. Joints for box construction: (a) rebated, or lapped: (b) comb, or finger; and (c) tongued

the end of the wood will be correspondingly reduced and consequently weakened.

Other corner joints include the plain mitre, the tongued mitre and the dowelled mitre. Dowels can also be used where the ends of the wood are left square.

What is a butt joint?

A butt joint is where neither piece of wood forming the joint is cut in any way, and thus there is no interlocking effect whatsoever. The joint therefore relies on glue, or glue used with nails, screws, or other items of hardware.

Two types of butt joints are shown in Fig. 56. That at (a) is used for widening purposes, for which the mating edges must be

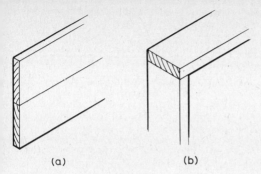

Fig. 56. *Butt joints (see text)*

planed absolutely true. Properly prepared and glued, the joint is at least as strong as the remainder of the wood. The butt joint at (b) is another variety of corner joint, and although glue can be used, it has limited holding power in this type of application. This is because the surface of one piece forming the joint is totally end grain, where the strength of any glue is very much reduced.

What determines the diameter of dowelling in dowel joints?

There are no hard and fast rules about the diameter of dowelling where joints are based on this material. As a general guide, though, the diameter of the dowel should be about half that of the wood being jointed. In practice, most dowel joints are based on dowelling with a diameter of between 6 mm (¼ in) and 13 mm (½ in).

How should the holes be spaced in a dowel joint?

This depends on the particular type of joint, and the size of the material involved. Where dowels are used to reinforce a butt joint as used for widening purposes, they are usually spaced at about

100 mm–150 mm (4 in–6 in). With framing-type joints, for material around 50 mm–75 mm (2 in–3 in) wide, two dowels should be used; for material which is about 100 mm (4 in) wide, three dowels are needed, and when the width is 125 mm–150 mm (5 in–6 in), four dowels are used.

Dowelling is an excellent method of jointing for man-made boards, and especially chipboard. For this purpose, the dowels are spaced at around 50 mm (2 in) centres.

Dowels should never be positioned too near the edge of the wood, since splitting can occur. As an approximate guide, the distance between the dowel and the edge of the material should equal the diameter of the dowel. In chipboard, dowels should not be positioned nearer than 20 mm (¾ in) to the edge of the wood.

How are dowel holes usually prepared?

Their positions are normally marked by pencil and gauge, although simple home-made marking aids can be used. Boring the holes can be by brace and bit, using a Jennings' pattern twist bit, or ideally a 'dowel bit', or they may be bored with a power drill. This can be used freehand, or in a stand, and used in conjunction with a lip-and-spur bit.

However, largely because of the popularity of chipboard and the suitability of dowelling for this material, there is a wide range of dowelling jigs on the market to facilitate the preparation of this joint. These range from very simple devices which allow for the boring of one hole of fixed size at one setting, to the fairly sophisticated 'Record 147' which caters for a number of sizes, and for multiple holes to be made at one setting. The better the quality of the jig, the less need there is to mark-out individual holes.

How are joints secured?

Most joints in woodwork are glued, and many are then strengthened by additional means. Nails and pins are used, and also screws for example on half-laps and bridle. Mortice and tenons are often secured by wedges, especially on joinery work;

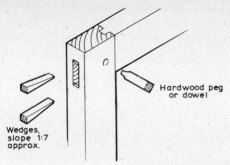

Fig. 57. *Wedging and pegging of mortice and tenons*

and for heavy constructions, pegs are frequently used as well (see Fig. 57). The pegs may be of dowelling, or hardwood of square section. On windows, the joints are often locked by driving in metal pins of star section.

Are fittings an acceptable alternative to conventional jointing methods?

During the last few years or so, a wide assortment of fittings has been introduced to act as alternatives to traditional jointing methods. Many of these have been designed for what is known as 'knock-down' furniture, and are referred to as 'KD' fittings. Their main purpose is to enable furniture to be sold unassembled in cartons, with usually a screwdriver and a hammer the only tools needed to assemble the components. KD fittings can of course be used where the furniture or other item is not specifically designed as KD.

Hardware used for jointing purposes includes a development of the wood screw which is part dowel and part screw, various metal angle plates used for strengthening the corner of assemblies, and the 'Scan' type of fitting which is based on the principle of the nut and bolt. Most fittings used for jointing purposes leave visible evidence of their use, although the majority are quite neat and are arranged to be on inner surfaces.

71

5
Constructions

Is a bevel the same as a chamfer?

No, although there is an element of similarity between them. A bevel is where the whole of the edge is formed at an angle other than 90°. A chamfer is where the corner only is removed. Although chamfers are frequently made at 45°, they can be at any angle. Chamfers have been much used in the past as decorative features, from Jacobean furniture to farm carts.

What is the difference between a groove and a trench?

Again the terms are similar; the difference relates to the direction of grain. A trench is cut across the grain, while a groove is formed along the grain. The different names probably arise from the fact that, when formed entirely by hand, the methods of cutting them have little in common. This is because of the directional nature of the fibres which form the grain, and thus different techniques are needed according to whether the wood is being worked across or along the grain.

What is a rebate, and how is it formed?

A rebate is shown in Fig. 58, and may be with or across the grain. Originally rebates were cut with a sash fillister plane. These were a special pattern of rebate plane fitted with a depth stop and a

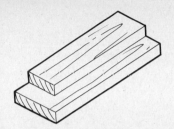

Fig. 58. A rebate

fence which controlled the depth and width of the rebate. Because these planes, and their present-day equivalents, were fitted with a side knife or spur, they could cut across the grain.

Rebates can also be cut in other ways, including: (a) using a standard-type rebate plane and with battens fixed to the wood to guide the plane; (b) on a circular saw, by making two cuts from adjacent surfaces until they meet; (c) on a planing machine equipped with facilities for rebating; (d) on a spindle moulding machine; (e) using an electric router; and (f) using a rebating attachment (a device which is in effect a very small circular saw) in a power drill.

Is a mitre always at 45°?

Although the commonest form of mitre is where the two pieces are both cut at 45° to make a combined angle of 90°, this is not always the case. Fig. 59(a) shows how the pieces must be cut to

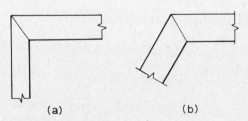

(a)   (b)

Fig. 59. Mitres other than 45° (see text)

73

form 90° if they are not of equal width, and (b) illustates two pieces mitred to a combined angle other than a right angle.

A mitre can also be curved, and this applies where one piece is itself curved, and the other straight or of different curvature to the first.

What are the main types of woodwork construction?

There are three main types: (a) flat frame, (b) stool, and (c) box. A flat-frame construction is of two-dimensional form – apart, that is, from the thickness of the wood making up the assembly. Doors and windows are examples of flat-frame construction. Stool construction is of a three-dimensional nature, and most tables come into this category. The material used for both flat-frame and stool construction is relatively narrow.

Box construction is where the assembly is made from material which is fairly wide compared with its thickness, that is wood which in most cases would be classed as boards. Items of furniture such as wardrobes, bookcases and sideboards are invariably of box construction, as well as drawers.

A piece of furniture like a blanket chest may be of box or stool construction, while others like, for example, a sideboard may be a combination of box for the main carcase, and stool for the supporting underframing.

What is a battened door?

A battened door is shown in Fig. 60. This type of door is a fairly simple piece of joinery, and is used for such applications as outhouses and garden sheds. The vertical boards are tongued and grooved together, and in most cases for 'full size' doors, three ledges are employed. The sloping members are known as braces, and add a very great deal of rigidity to the door although they are not always included. The braces make the door 'handed'. This means the side on which the door is hung cannot be changed, since for the braces to be effective they must slope upwards from

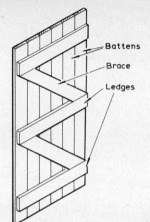

Battens

Brace

Ledges

Fig. 60. *Ledged, braced and battened door*

the hanging edge. Joints are not used with this type of door; instead it is nailed together usually with oval nails which are then bent over or 'clenched' when they penetrate the battens.

Battened doors are also used in 'cottage'-type properties for built-in cupboards. Lightweight versions can also be used on furniture of the traditional type, such as dressers.

What is a raised panel, and how are panels held in place?

A raised panel is one where the centre part of the panel projects further forwards than the outer part. This is shown in the left-hand side of the sectional drawing illustrated in Fig. 61. The

Fig. 61. *Sections through raised panels*

right-hand side of the section shows a variation on a simple raised panel known as raised and fielded. Alternative ways of shaping and forming raised panels are possible, and such panels are invariably made in solid wood.

75

Panels, whether of solid wood or plywood, are normally held in their frames in grooves, also shown in Fig. 61. Note that with solid wood panels, they must never be a tight fit within the grooves, but must have a space left at the bottom of the groove. This is to allow the panel to expand and contract according to seasonal and other changes, and for this reason solid panels must never be glued in place. Incorrectly-fitted solid panels are very likely to lead to the development of faults at a later date. Ply panels will neither shrink nor swell, and therefore the precautions regarding fitting are less demanding.

How is the glass held in place in a small cabinet door?

Fig. 62 shows a section through a small glazed door. The inner edge of the door is rebated into which the glass is fitted, then it is held in position by glazing beads. The beads are mitred at the

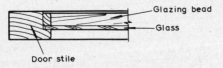

Fig. 62. *How glass is held in small glazed door*

corners, and secured either by pins or small screws. Typical depth of rebate is 8 mm (5/16 in), and the thickness of the beads should equal this thickness for a neat job.

For very superior work, strips of chamois leather should be glued into the rebates. This provides a slightly resilient bedding for the glass, and on cabinet work is preferred to putty.

What is the standard construction for a drawer?

The commonest method of making drawers is shown in Fig. 63. Lap dovetails are used at the front, and through dovetails at the

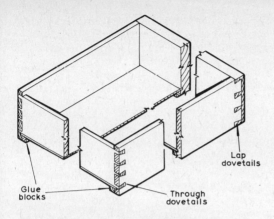

Fig. 63. *Typical drawer construction*

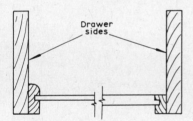

Fig. 64. *Use of drawer slips*

rear. The usual material for the drawer bottom is plywood. Hardboard can also be used, but tends to sag after a period of time. Solid wood is still used on top-class work. The bottom is usually held in grooves in the front and sides, but is secured to the lower edge of the back. This allows the bottom to be inserted after the rest of the drawer is assembled. Glue blocks are often added to the underside; these not only strengthen the drawer, they effectively widen the surface on which the drawer runs.

77

Drawer bottoms can also be held in place by using 'drawer slips', of which two variations are shown in Fig. 64. These also increase the bearing surface on which the drawer slides.

What other methods are used for making drawers?

There are a number of variations in the way in which drawers are made:

1. The corners may be slot-dovetailed together as shown in plan in Fig. 65(a). The trenches should be stopped so as to be concealed when the drawer is opened. This method can only be used where the design is such that the front of the drawer extends beyond the sides.

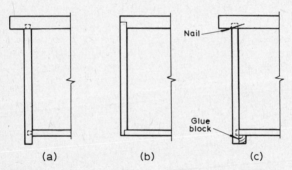

(a) (b) (c)

Fig. 65. *Alternative joints for drawers: (a) dovetail trenched, (b) rebated, and (c) trenched*

2. The front and back can be rebated to give the joint shown at (b). This is only suitable for small drawers because of limited strength.
3. The parts may be trenched together, as in (c). These trenches should be stopped, and again the strength is far less than a dovetailed drawer. The joints at the front should be nailed as shown, while a glue block at the rear adds to the strength.

4. Comb joints may be used, with a lap arranged on those at the front. In practice, this is not a joint which would be chosen to be cut by hand, but becomes a viable method if a box combing jig for use with a power drill is available.

What is a 'false front' to a drawer?

A false front is where the front of the drawer as seen is added as a separate part once the four main components are assembled. It means that making and fitting the drawer are simplified a little, as through dovetails can be used throughout. False fronts are more applicable where the design is such that the drawer front overlaps the carcase, rather than fitting within it.

How are drawers supported within a cabinet?

A drawer is supported on its underside by a component known as the runner. This should always be of hardwood to resist wear, and must be sufficiently wide to support the drawer side plus the blocks or slips.

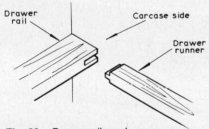

Fig. 66. *Drawer rails and runners*

Where the carcase includes a drawer rail or rails, it is preferable to incorporate a stub mortice and tenon between the rail and the runner. This is shown in Fig. 66, the runner being fixed to the side of the carcase by screws. If the carcase side is of solid wood, then the screws must be 'slotted'.

The kicker is the component which controls the top of the drawer, and ensures it opens without tilting forward. In a nest of drawers, the runner of one drawer acts as the kicker to the one below. A single drawer, or the top one of a nest, must be provided with a kicker. This is very similar to a runner, but need not be as wide. The kicker is often used, additionally, to partly support the top of a unit.

Sometimes, and especially where a table is being fitted with a drawer, the inner surface of the drawer aperture is not level because of the way the legs and rails are arranged. In these cases, strips of wood known as drawer guides must be added to the aperture in order to make this surface flush.

Is there a simple method of supporting drawers?

A simplified method of supporting and guiding drawers is used a great deal in commercial woodwork. The drawer sides are grooved about the centre of their outer surface, the groove being stopped just short of the front. The grooves are made about 19 mm (¾ in) wide, with pieces of wood of the same thickness being added to the inside of the carcase and so arranged that the drawer can slide on them. Thus these two members act as runners, kickers and guides, but this apparently simple system suffers from a major drawback.

Inevitably, the depth of the groove which can be made on the drawer side is very limited. This in turn, especially when a little has to be allowed for clearance, means that the amount of surface bearing the weight of the drawer is extremely limited. With this method of construction, drawers which are in constant use soon wear at the top edge of the side groove which is where the weight is taken.

What is meant by a plinth to a cabinet?

A plinth is normally taken as being a separately constructed base on which a piece of furniture stands. It is usually of box construction, and secured to the main carcase by screw-blocks or

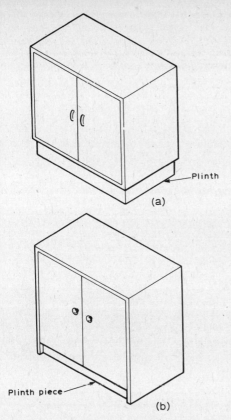

Fig. 67. *Cabinet with (a) separate plinth, (b) plinth piece*

angle plates. It is shown in Fig. 67(a). An alternative to having a separate plinth is to have the arrangement illustrated at (b), where the filler piece at the lower front might be loosely referred to as a plinth.

81

How are backs secured to cabinets?

Although in top-class work the back of a piece of furniture is often a panelled framework, in most cases it is made of plywood. For kitchen units, white-face hardboard is invariably used.

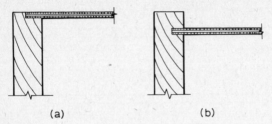

Fig. 68. *Methods of fixing backs: (a) rebated, and (b) grooved*

There are two principal ways of securing backs, and these are shown in Fig. 68. (a) shows a rebate, where the back is fixed by screws or round-head nails. Grooving the back in place is illustrated at (b). Normal procedure with this method is to groove the sides and top, with the base reduced in width so that the back can be slid upwards into place after the main parts have been assembled. The back is then secured to the rear edge of the base.

Only in the cheapest and simplest of work is the back secured directly to the rear edges of the carcase without either grooving or rebating.

How is a table top fixed?

The method of fixing depends to some extent on the material from which the top is made, the size of the table, and the nature of the underframing.

If the top is of solid wood, provision has to be made for shrinking and swelling, usually simply referred to as 'movement'. If a solid top is rigidly secured to its underframing, either it is likely to swell and cause distortion, or even more likely shrink and split as a result.

The time-honoured method of securing a table top is to use 'buttons'. An example is shown in Fig. 69, being about 38 mm × 32 mm × 19 mm (1½ in × 1¼ in × ¾ in), the tongue of which engages in a shallow mortice in the side rail. The mortice is cut slightly longer than the width of the button, enabling it to move either sideways, a little, or in and out of the mortice, depending on the direction of grain of the top.

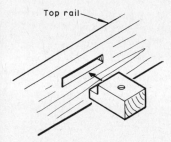
Top rail

Fig. 69. Wooden 'button'

Solid tops are now often secured with metal plates known as expansion plates. These have slotted holes for the screws to allow for movement.

Table tops made of man-made boards such as chip or blockboard are not subject to movement, and therefore can be more rigidly fixed. Screw blocks can be used, or the top can be fixed by screws which pass right through the side rails, usually by the method known as counterboring. Man-made tops can of course be fixed by buttons or expansion plates.

What is a glue block?

This is shown in Fig. 70, and is usually between 13 mm (½ in) and 19 mm (¾ in) square, with lengths up to 76 mm (3 in). Glue blocks are used to add strength to the inner corner of a joint where they will not normally be seen. The tiny chamfer is a refinement which allows for better 'bedding', as does the fairly

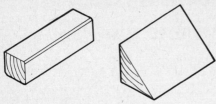

Fig. 70. Glue blocks

short length, and when spaced-out also provides for movement when used across the grain of solid material. Glue blocks can also be made to triangular section.

Glue blocks are often added to the underside of drawers.

What is a screw block?

A screw block is similar to a glue block, but usually made in a continuous length. Holes are prepared along adjacent faces so that the block can be screwed in two directions for securing or strengthening purposes.

Where a screw block is fixed across the grain of solid wood, then the holes for the screws must be elongated, this being known as slot-screwing.

6
Nails, screws and glue

What are the commonest types of nails in regular use?

The three commonest patterns of nails are shown in Fig. 71, and
are the round head, oval, and panel pin. Nails are manufactured
from wire, with round heads and ovals made in lengths from
20 mm–150 mm (¾ in–6 in), with longer ones produced as

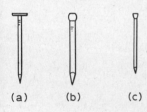

Fig. 71. *Nails in common use:
(a) round-headed, (b) oval, and
(c) panel pin*

specials. Panel pins are made from 13 mm–50 mm (½ in–2 in).
The gauge of the nail relates to its diameter, and this is now
simply expressed in millimetres.

When should round-heads be used, as opposed to ovals?

Round-head nails are used a great deal in constructional
(carpentry) type of work, where there is an actual 'load' carried
by the nail. A typical example of this is in roofing work. The large
head helps to resist the separation of the parts being secured, and
therefore round-heads should be used whenever the nail becomes

85

a load-bearing component of the structure, and where the visible head is of no consequence.

Ovals have fairly slender heads which are intended to be punched below the surface of the wood, and the hole to be subsequently 'filled' so as to conceal the location of the nail. A direct strain on an oval nail can result in it being pulled completely through the wood, as the small head offers little resistance. Oval nails are used where the direct pull on the nail is minimal, such as for securing skirting boards and door frames, and for lighter work generally.

Small, light-gauge round-head nails are also used for securing ply and hardboard onto frames, especially if the boards are fairly thin, and the nails will not be visible.

What is a clout nail, and where is it used?

Clout nails have very large heads, and are usually supplied with a galvanised finish to resist rusting. Made in lengths from 20 mm (¾ in) up to 100 mm (4 in), the shorter ones are used for securing roofing felt, and the longer ones for fixing tiles and slates. Clout nails are also known as slate nails. The large heads of these nails make them suitable for fixing fairly soft materials such as cork, strawboard, and other insulation boards. There is also a type of clout nail with an extra-large head.

What metals are nails usually made of?

The overwhelming majority of nails are made from mild steel. Nails are also made in brass, copper, and gunmetal, and these are used particularly in the boat-building industry. Nails for securing roof-cladding materials are also produced in aluminium.

In addition, nails are produced with various finishes. As well as the galvanised variety, they are manufactured in a sheradised finish which also provides rust resistance. Decorative nails are produced with electroplated finishes in brass or bronze, and the small nails known as gimp pins are available in a range of painted finishes.

What is dovetail nailing?

This is shown in Fig. 72, and is used particularly where the nails are driven into end grain. Because of the cellular structure of

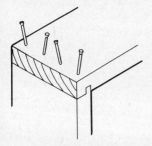

Fig. 72. Dovetail nailing

timber, nails do not grip as well in end grain as side grain, but by slanting the nails this grip is improved.

What is meant by clenching nails?

This is where the nail chosen is long enough to penetrate through the member being nailed by about 16 mm (⅝ in), then the protruding end is bent over and punched below the surface. It is shown in section in Fig. 73.

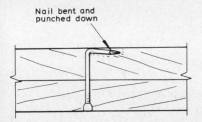

Fig. 73. Clenching nails

This method of nailing is used where the piece being nailed into is relatively thin, and where therefore shorter nails would not have sufficient holding power. Clenching is used in simpler types of joinery work, such as battened doors.

Why are nails punched in?

The usual reason for punching nails below the suface is to conceal their presence. The small hole left after punching is filled level with the surface of the wood to disguise the nail. For work which is to be given a clear finish, fillers, or stoppers, are used to match the colour of the wood. For work to be painted, putty or a plaster-based filler can be used.

How can wood be prevented from splitting when nailing?

Dodges which are used include:

1. Pre-boring for the nails. This is a useful method where the wood is quite hard, the holes being made approximately two-thirds the diameter of the nail. This technique is also employed where nailing is taking place near the end of the wood, since this area is particularly vulnerable to splitting.
2. Again where nailing is near the end of the material, do not cut the wood to its required length until *after* nailing.
3. 'Stagger' the position of the nails. Do not place a series of nails in a straight line along the grain, as the cumulative effect of a number of nails so positioned can cause splitting.

What nails are used in upholstery work?

The three nails which are particularly associated with upholstery are shown in Fig. 74. The tack, or cut tack (a), usually has a blued finish, and an extremely sharp point. Made in various lengths up to 25 mm (1 in), they are used for securing webbing, hessian and other materials where the tack will subsequently be covered.

The dome-headed upholstery nail (b) has a head diameter around 10 mm ($\frac{3}{8}$ in), with lengths from 13 mm–19 mm ($\frac{1}{2}$ in–$\frac{3}{4}$ in). This is a decorative type of nail, usually with a brassed or bronzed finish.

88

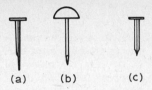

Fig. 74. Nails used for upholstery: (a) cut tack, (b) dome-headed, and (c) gimp pin

The gimp pin (c) normally has a square shank and a small round head, with lengths from 10 mm–25 mm (⅜ in–1 in). This type is used for fixing braid and for securing covering fabrics, especially the backs of upholstered pieces.

What is a staple?

A staple is a form of nail, U-shaped with both ends pointed. Its size ranges from 13 mm–50 mm (½ in–2 in), and it invariably has a galvanised finish. Staples are used a great deal in fencing work, for securing both wire and wire netting.

What is a countersunk screw?

This is a screw with a flat head, the underside of which is splayed at 45° towards the shank. The head is intended to be flush with the surface of the wood, or face of the fitting, when driven in. A hole for a countersunk screw must itself be countersunk so as to properly accommodate the head. Countersunk screws are the commonest type of screws in general use.

What are the differences between a round-head and a raised-head screw?

There are two differences. The underside of the head on a round head screw is flat, and the height of the head is approximately two thirds its diameter. With a raised-head screw, the underside of the head is of countersunk form, and the height of the domed part of the head is around one third its diameter.

How is the size of a screw measured?

Screws are measured in two ways, are ascertained in Imperial dimensions and look like remaining this way a long time after the general introduction of metrication. The length is stated in inches and fractions of an inch, and is measured up to the part of the head which finishes level with the surface of the work. Thus for a countersunk screw, the stated length of the screw is the actual overall length of the screw, whereas for both raised- and round-heads the length is taken from the tip to the lower edge of the dome of the head.

The diameter of the screw is measured by what is known as the screw gauge. The gauge ranges from 0–20, the most popular ones being from 2s–10s.

The gauge can be ascertained by measuring the head, which is always twice the diameter of the shank. If the diameter of the head is measured in thirty-seconds of an inch, and two then deducted from this, the result is the gauge of the screw. For example, a screw head has a diameter of $3/8$ in, or $12/32$ in. Deducting two from this gives the gauge as 10. To work out the diameter from the gauge, simply reverse the procedure, so for example a number 6 screw will have a head with a diameter of $6 + 2/32$ in = $8/32$ in or $1/4$ in.

What metals are screws normally made of?

By far the most common metal used for screws is mild steel. Screws are also made in brass, aluminium alloy, stainless steel, and silicon bronze. There has been a trend in recent years to offer steel screws with a bright zinc plating, which helps resist rusting and also provides for easier driving.

Screws can also be obtained with various finishes, such as chrome, brassed, and sheradised. Screws with a glossy black enamel (Japanned) finish are also produced.

Note that not every type of metal or finish can be obtained over the full range of sizes.

What screws should be used where the risk of rusting is high?

Brass, aluminium alloy, stainless steel and silicon bronze are all rust-resisting. Stainless steel and silicon bronze are usually used to secure fittings of the the same metal, especially for the fitting-out of boats. Brass screws are used for more general work where water is present, and are used for wood-to-wood fixings on boats.

Certain woods corrode steel, because of their acidic nature. Both oak and chestnut are of this type, and brass screws should always be used in these timbers.

What is a coach screw?

A coach screw is a very heavy-duty screw, and is provided with a square head which enables a spanner to be used to drive it home. They are used where the screw itself is taking a considerable load, and are produced in sizes from 1 in × ¼ in–6 in × ½ in diameter.

Coach screws are manufactured in mild steel, with a limited range also available with a heavy bright zinc plating.

What is a twinfast screw?

Whereas a conventional screw has a single thread, twinfast screws have a double or twin thread. They are used particularly in low- and medium-density chipboards, and in softwoods, and because of the twin thread they are driven into the wood in half the time of conventional screws.

Less preparation of the wood is required when using twinfast screws, and the risk of the material splitting is reduced. The smaller sizes of these screws are threaded right up to the head. This gives increased holding power where the screw is used to secure a fitting, and where, therefore, almost all the screw enters the wood to form the anchor.

Assuming the screws are being used for wood-to-wood fixing, the first piece of material needs to be bored for the shank of the screw. This is shown at (a) in Fig. 75, and is known as the clearance hole. It should have the same diameter as the shank of the screw, or be very close indeed to this dimension.

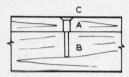

Fig. 75. *Preparing wood for screws*

The piece which is being screwed into also requires boring. This is called the pilot hole, and is shown at (b). The diameter of this hole should be approximately half that of the clearance hole, with its depth approximating to the length of the screw.

If the screw is of the countersunk type, then the clearance hole needs to be countersunk so that the head of the screw when inserted will be flush with the surface. Countersinking is shown at (c).

Engineer's morse-type drills are excellent for preparing wood for screws, as is a countersink drill normally intended for metalworking. When securing fittings to wood, the only preparation required is making the pilot holes. Pilot holes for small screws are usually made with a bradawl.

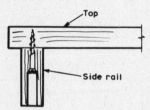

Fig. 76. *Counterboring a screw*

What is meant by counterboring?

Counterboring is where the whole of the head of the screw is recessed into a hole made for it. It is shown in Fig. 76, and is usually employed where the screw has to pass through a fairly wide piece of wood, to avoid using an excessively long screw. An example of its use is shown where the top of a small table has been secured to a side rail.

How can screw heads be concealed?

For furniture and similar work, screws are normally located where they will be out of sight. When a screw is on a visible surface, it can be counterbored, and the hole filled with a 'pellet' of similar wood cut with the grain to match its surroundings. For simple work where screws are used in a visible position, a variety of plastic screw caps are available. They conceal the screws, but are themselves visible, of course.

What is a suitable adhesive for general woodworking?

The most popular and versatile adhesive for a wide variety of woodworking applications is polyvinyl acetate. Known as PVA, it is a white emulsion, is used cold, and is bought ready for use. It is produced by a large number of manufacturers and is widely available. It will bond most materials associated with woodworking, including cork, fabrics, leather and tiles. It is not waterproof, and must be protected from frost, which changes its characteristics.

What glues can be used for outdoor work?

Only glues which are classed as being waterproof can be used for outdoor woodwork. They are loosely known as 'resin' glues, and two of the most popular types are 'Cascamite-one-Shot', and

'Areolite 306'. The former is bought as a powder, and mixed as required with water to a fairly thick consistency, then applied to the work. The hardening agent is already mixed with the powder, and is activated when wet.

Areolite 306 is a two-part adhesive. The powder is mixed with water, and applied to one part of the work. The hardener, or catalyst, is a clear liquid and is applied to the second surface to be joined. Setting only takes place when the two surfaces, suitably coated, are brought together.

Both these adhesives have been well-tested, and are suitable for such demanding work as boat-building.

What is a contact adhesive?

Most contact adhesives are rubber-based, and are particularly used for bonding plastic laminates onto a suitable base or ground. In use, the adhesive is spread onto both surfaces, left for a few minutes, then the work brought together. The bond is almost instantaneous, making realignment of the work (should this be needed) almost impossible. Full strength is reached after several hours. Impact adhesives are waterproof, but are not suitable for general assembly work.

7
Fittings and hardware

What is a Scan-type screw?

This is shown in Fig. 77. Lengths are up to 76 mm (3 in), with a diameter of 6 mm (¼ in). The head has a hexagonal socket to allow for tightening with an Allen key. The cross-dowel part of the fitting is made in three lengths from 14 mm–25 mm (⁹⁄₁₆ in–1 in).

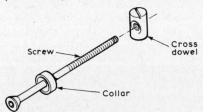

Fig. 77. *Scan-type screw*

Scan screws and cross-dowels can be used as an alternative to formal joints, or they can be used to reinforce a joint such as a mortice and tenon. They allow the assembly to be dismantled fairly readily, and so are classed as a 'knock-down' (KD) fitting. Finish is usually electro-brassed, or blacked.

What are connecting screws used for?

As their name suggests, these screws are used to fasten together unit pieces of furniture, or kitchen units, so as to make a composite whole. They are so designed that they appear to have a 'head' at both ends thus giving a neat appearance. The actual screw is of metal, with the end parts of white, brown or beige plastic.

Are screw-on 'bloc'-type jointing methods as good as traditional joints?

Corner 'bloc' joints are most frequently used in conjunction with veneered chipboard, and chipboard does not lend itself to many of the traditional joints which were evolved for solid wood. However, chipboard can be dowel-jointed in most instances, this offering a strong method which is also completely concealed on assembly. Screwed corner blocs have the advantage of simplicity, making them attractive where speed or limited facilities have to be considered. They are also useful where the work needs to be de-mountable, as the two halves of the fitting are easily separated. On the other hand, they are neither as neat, nor as strong, as a dowelled joint.

What is the purpose of a corner bracket?

Corner brackets are used for squaring-up and strengthening assemblies, and especially for cabinets and wall units. They are

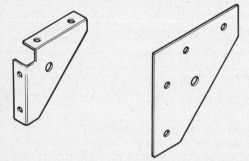

Fig. 78. Corner brackets

normally of steel with a zinc-plated finish, and are provided with a central hole to enable cabinets to be secured to the wall. Two patterns are shown in Fig. 78, the left-hand one also being made in white polypropylene.

These brackets can also be used for purposes of strengthening and securing other than at corners.

What are concealed hinges?

Concealed pattern hinges have a cylindrical barrel which is recessed into and secured to the inner face of the door, with the arms from this being pivoted to a plate which in turn is secured to the inner face of the carcase. They are made in patterns to open 95° or greater, either all-metal or part white or brown plastic. They are also made either plain, or spring-loaded. With the latter, the spring holds the door in the open position, or in the closed position, thus eliminating the need for a separate door catch.

While these hinges are essentially easy to fix, they do require the accurate boring of a blind hole to accommodate the barrel. They are completely hidden when the doors are closed, and have the great advantage over other hinges in that they allow for limited adjustment once the doors are located on the cabinet.

The standard size of barrel for these hinges is 35 mm ($1\frac{2}{5}$ in) diameter, but a mini-version is also made with a diameter of 26 mm (1 in).

What are lay-on hinges?

Although these hinges are also completely hidden when the door is closed, they should not be confused with the 'concealed' hinge as described above. No recessing of any type is required for this cabinet hinge, it simply 'lays-on' the inner surfaces of the door and carcase. They are made in steel with a nickel-plated finish, and are available either sprung or unsprung. Produced in one size only of approximately 105 mm × 44 mm (4 in × $1\frac{4}{5}$ in) when open, they can be used for doors which fit within the cabinet sides, or on the face of the carcase.

What is the difference between a butt hinge and a back-flap hinge?

The main difference between these hinges is in the proportion of the two main parts of the hinge which are called the leaves. Whereas the butt hinge has relatively narrow leaves, the width of the back flap leaves is a little greater than the length of the hinge.

The main purpose of the back-flap hinge is to provide extra strength by enabling the fixing screws to be positioned well away from the knuckle, and therefore the edge of the work. The common use of butt hinges is for doors, where the relative thinness of most doors restricts the width of hinge which can be used.

Both these patterns of hinge are made in pressed steel, pressed brass, and solid brass. They are also made with an electro-brassed finish. Larger sizes of butt hinges are produced in cast iron, aluminium, and even nylon. Better-quality hinges of the larger sizes have steel washers between the knuckles to lessen wear.

A large butt hinge with a wide leaf which is usually of decorative shape is often used for hanging heavy entrance doors. Known as Parliament hinges, they are used where the doors open through 180°, and the wide hinge enables the doors to clear the architraves.

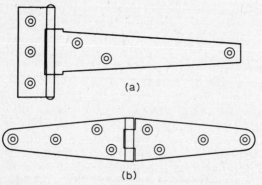

Fig. 79. *(a) Tee, and (b) strap hinges*

When is a strap hinge used as opposed to a T-hinge?

A T-hinge is shown in Fig. 79(a), and is mainly used for hanging doors of sheds, garages and outbuildings where the frame of the structure will only allow for the narrow part of the hinge to be accommodated. The strap hinge (Fig. 79*b*) can only be used where there is unrestricted space to allow the hinge to be fixed. Strap hinges are often used for the lids of large storage boxes.

Both these patterns of hinge are almost always made in pressed steel, and either have a Japanned finish or are left self-coloured.

What are bands and gudgeons?

Bands and gudgeons are the two components which make up a very heavy-duty hinge. They are shown in Fig. 80; examples of their use include garage doors and garden gates.

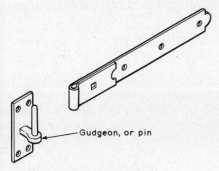

Gudgeon, or pin

Fig. 80. *Band and gudgeon*

Made in mild steel and left self-coloured, they are produced in a wide range of sizes. The bands have a square hole as shown in Fig. 80 to enable a coach bolt to be used at this point, the remainder of the fixing being by screws.

The gudgeon, or pin, is made with different types of fixing to the plate shown. These include a single heavy bolt, and steel wings for building into brickwork.

What is a flush hinge?

The flush hinge, also known as the Hurlinge, is shown in Fig. 81. Its main use is for hanging doors. Because of the way in which one leaf fits within the other, it is not necessary to form any recesses for this hinge, as the thickness of the leaf provides the clearance.

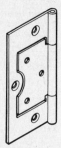

Fig. 81. *Flush hinge*

Flush hinges are made in sizes up to 100 mm (4 in) with a variety of finishes.

This hinge is also made with a loose pin, thus enabling a door to be removed without withdrawing the fixing screws.

What is a mortice lock?

A mortice lock is usually used on domestic and other doors as a security lock. The lock fits in a recess, or mortice, within the thickness of the door, making it both invisible and inaccessible when the door is closed.

Terminology can be confusing with this pattern of lock. A mortice lock combines a spring latch, operated by handle, as well as the bolt operated by key. A mortice dead-lock has the bolt only, and no spring latch.

For good security protection, the lock should be of the three-lever pattern, and preferably of five-lever. The part of the lock which is secured to the frame is known as the striking plate, or striking box if of the enclosed type.

What is a window stay?

A window stay is the fitting which controls the amount by which a window is opened, and which holds it in the open position. For small, top-hung sashes, the window stay also holds the window in the closed position. For larger, side-hung sashes, the window is additionally held closed by a 'window fastener'.

Is there a simple way of supporting shelving within a cabinet?

A number of simple fittings are available; a selection is shown in Fig. 82. That at (a) is made in white or brown plastic, the stud part clipping into the sleeve. The one at (b) is metal with a plated finish, and this is very unobtrusive with the support being a press fit in the sleeve.

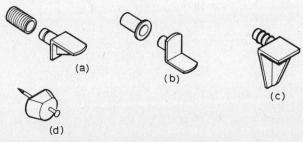

(a)

(b)

(c)

(d)

Fig. 82. *Shelf-support fittings: (a) two-part plastic, (b) two-part metal, (c) one-piece plastic, and (d) plastic with moulded-in nail*

Both the above lend themselves to a system of adjustable shelving, by having rows of sleeves suitably spaced.

The plastic one illustrated at (c) is produced in white, brown or beige. Here, the one-piece fitting is simply inserted into a blind hole.

That at (d) is extremely simple, the plastic button being held by the pin which is built-in during manufacture. This is only really suitable for small shelves such as, for example, in a bathroom cabinet.

What are extruded handles?

These handles get their name from the manufacturing process by which they are produced. Made in aluminium, the process produces long lengths of handle of a given section, of which a selection is shown in Fig. 83. They are normally fitted across the

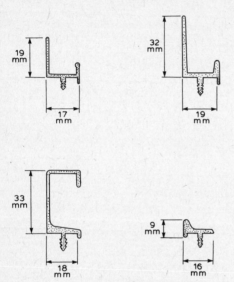

Fig. 83. *Sections of extruded handles*

full width of a door or drawer, and may be added to either the top or bottom edge. They are secured by inserting the barbed tongue into a suitably prepared groove, with a little adhesive added to provide a good bond.

These handles are used extensively on kitchen units. Handles which are similar to the aluminium ones are also produced in plastic.

Can a drawer be made entirely out of plastic?

Yes; there are a number of plastic drawer systems on the market. The drawer side profile is made in various widths, or depths, and incorporates a groove on the inside for the drawer bottom, and one on the outside to engage with the runner which is secured to the carcase side. Corner fittings enable the parts to be assembled; these usually work by cementing the components together, or by spring clips. The drawer front is made out of the same material as the remainder of the piece, while white-faced hardboard is the usual material for the drawer bottom.

What are expansion plates?

An expansion plate is shown in Fig. 84. They are made in mild steel with a plated finish, typical sizes being 38 mm × 25 mm × 25 mm (1½ in × 1 in × 1 in). They were originally introduced as an alternative to traditional buttons for

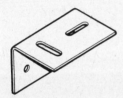

Fig. 84. Angle expansion plate

securing table tops to an underframing. They are screwed in place, and by using whichever slot is at right-angles to the grain of the top, swelling and shrinkage are allowed for. Although such provision for movement is only needed with solid wood, these plates can also be used where the table top is of man-made board.

Expansion plates can also be used for securing plinths to cabinets, and for general securing purposes.

What is a coach bolt, and what is its purpose?

A coach bolt has a fairly large domed head, immediately below this is a square shank which extends about 6 mm (¼ in). the thread is normally of 'Whitworth' form, and extends only part-way along the length of the bolt. The bolt is provided with a square nut. Coach bolts are normally given a blackened finish.

Coach bolts are made specially for use with wood, either for wood-to-wood fastening where considerable strength is required, or where heavy fittings such as bands and gudgeons are being fitted. The square part below the head either engages with the square hole usually provided in the fitting, or bites into the wood, in both cases the purpose being to prevent the bolt from rotating while the nut is being tightened. A washer should always be used beneath the nut.

8
Cleaning-up and assembling

Why is it so important to 'clean-up' a piece of woodwork before applying a surface finish?

The quality of the finish given to a piece of woodwork is dependent not just on the finish itself, but on the surface to which it is given. The idea that faults and imperfections are hidden during the finishing stages is a myth; in fact the opposite is true. Clear finishes in particular have a magnifying effect on the surface, and therefore minor blemishes and irregularities look even more pronounced once a surface coating has been applied. This is even more true with 'high gloss' finishes, and standard paints cannot be relied on to have complete obliterating powers.

The aims when carrying out the cleaning-up process include:

1. Levelling-off joints and adjoining surfaces.
2. Removing pencil and other marks.
3. Filling cracks and blemishes.
4. Making the surface sufficiently smooth according to the finish to be given. This includes removing the tell-tale traces of the work having been planed by hand, or the ripples produced during machine planing.
5. Removing all traces of glue if the work is to be given a clear finish.
6. Slightly rounding all sharp corners so as to improve the 'feel' of the object.

When does cleaning-up normally take place?

This can vary according to the nature and complexity of the work, but it is usually one of the latter operations. Inner surfaces which cannot be attended to once assembly takes place must be cleaned-up prior to assembly. Normally, outer surfaces are cleaned-up once all the parts are assembled, as this often includes levelling-off adjoining members.

Taking a panelled entrance door as an example, the surfaces of the panels, and the inner edges of the remaining parts making up the door, are all cleaned-up before assembly. This is because of relative inaccessibility to cleaning-up methods after assembly. The faces of the stiles, rails and muntins are not attended to until after assembly, since cleaning-up these surfaces prior to assembly would not ensure flush surfaces at the joints, and these would still have to be levelled later.

What is the purpose of a cabinet scraper?

It has two main purposes. It helps to rid the surface of the undulations and ridges left after planing, and is often more successful than a plane in smoothing areas where the grain is very irregular. The cutting action of a scraper is produced by the burr which is formed along its edges when sharpened (shown enlarged in Fig. 85). Softwoods do not respond well to scraping; generally

Fig. 85. *Enlarged view of scraper*

the harder the wood the better it can be scraped. Scrapers can be obtained which are held in a metal body, and where the cutting action can be adjusted, although all scraping techniques have to some extent been overtaken by power-sanding methods.

106

Why is glasspapering normally carried out along the grain?

All abrasive papers work by scratching the surface, with the coarser grits producing the larger scratches. When glasspapering takes place along the grain, these scratches blend in with the fibres which make up the grain pattern. Glasspapering across the grain, by contrast, severs the surface of the fibres, and does not conceal the scratches. Cross-grain glasspapering, especially if fairly coarse paper has been used, will show up if the work is given a clear finish.

Where the work is to be painted, it matters little which way glasspapering takes place. If the work consists of members with different grain directions, such as the frame shown in Fig. 86, then pieces 1 should be abraded before pieces 2. Proceeding in this sequence minimises the amount of cross grain abrading at the corners.

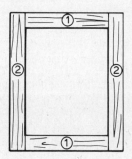

Fig. 86. *Sequence for using glasspaper: pieces (1) should be abraded before pieces (2)*

In veneered work such as marquetry where the grain of the many pieces can run in all directions, it is essential to use only very fine grades of paper. Even medium-grit paper could ruin work of this type, and may even cut right through the veneer.

What is flour paper?

Flour paper is the finest grade of abrasive paper made for general use, and is normally taken as being equal to grade 00. It is mostly used for smoothing-down between coats when a clear finish is being applied, and especially in high-class furniture work.

Is sand still used on abrasive paper?

Sand has never in fact been used as an abrading material. The popular idea that sharp sand bonded to paper backing was the first type of abrading paper is ill-founded. Crushed glass, graded according to the size of the particles, was the original material used, and is still popular because of its cheapness. Sandpaper and sanding are therefore misnomers.

What abrasives are normally used on abrasive paper?

As well as glass, the two other most-used abrasives are garnet and aluminous oxide. Garnet is a semi-precious stone, and its hard nature gives fast cutting, and it retains this property for a long period. Garnet papers are usually orange-coloured. Aluminous oxide is a multi-purpose abrasive, and is sufficiently hard to enable it to abrade a wide range of materials including metal, plastics and stone, as well as wood and also painted surfaces. Papers coated with aluminous oxide are usually brown or white.

Why is it important to use a block when hand sanding?

The main reason is that the flat surface of the block helps to produce a flat surface on the work. If held by the fingers, the paper would tend to follow any slight undulations, whereas when used with the block, abrading is initially concentrated on any 'high spots'. Using a block also enables a reasonable amount of pressure to be applied, which is important when sanding.

In addition, the block is also a more satisfactory way of ensuring that all parts of the work are covered, and also makes better use of the paper and extends its life. Glasspapering blocks

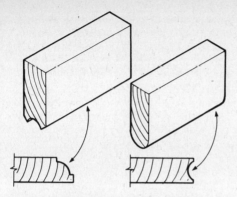

Fig. 87. Shaped glasspaper blocks

are also known as rubbers, and corks. The latter name is because they are often made from cork, or wood faced with cork.

For mouldings and other similar parts, shaped blocks should be made which are the reverse shape to the part to be sanded. Two simple examples are shown in Fig. 87; these are made from wood.

What is meant by the term 'rounding the arris'?

As part of the cleaning-up stage, it is usual to round-over all sharp corners. This makes the work pleasanter to handle, and lessens the risk of damage and bruising which a sharp corner is

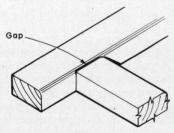

Gap

Fig. 88. Faulty rounding-off

vulnerable to. The amount of rounding is a matter of choice and circumstances. A man-made board with a veneered face and edge can only be lightly rounded, whereas solid wood can be more fully rounded. Light rounding is completed entirely by glasspaper; more extensive rounding is best preliminarily shaped by plane.

Care is needed not to round over an edge where an adjoining member abuts, or the result can be an ugly gap as shown in Fig. 88. According to the nature of the work, therefore, arrises are removed either before or after assembly.

What is meant by a 'dry run' when assembling?

A dry run is really a trial assembly. This is carried out to ensure that joints are not over-tight, that all parts of the joint have been fully cut, and that there are no restrictions to the work being assembled as planned. Very often joints can be individually fitted, and in many cases, dovetails for example, it is only necessary to partly assemble a joint to assess that all is well. It is wise to mark all the joints to ensure the parts are correctly assembled as intended, especially if there is a measure of individual fitting involved.

What tests should be applied to an assembly once cramped?

The following tests should be applied when the work is cramped, especially if glue has been used. Work which is faulty at the time of gluing is almost certain to remain so once the glue sets, making subsequent correction often impossible.
1. Testing for being square. For fairly small work, a try square can be used. For larger assemblies, the diagonals should be checked for being equal, either with a squaring lath, or a rule.
2. Testing for being flat, or out-of-twist. This is done by eye, by sighting across two opposite members to check that the edge of one is in line with the other. This should always be carried out with great care, as the tightening action of the cramps can induce 'twist' into a frame which was hitherto quite flat.
3. Testing for parallelism. This is important where the frame consists of three members only, such as for example the two

legs and rail of a table underframing. A cramp placed so as to exert pressure on the top rail can cause the lower ends of the legs to move either inwards or outwards.

At what stage of assembling are wedges, pegs, nails or screws added to the joints?

Wedges must be inserted at the time of actually cramping up, and these too are glued in place once all checks have been carried out. Pegs, nails and screws can be added at any time as convenient. However, if the strength of the assembly is very much dependent on these securing methods, then either they must be inserted immediately after cramping if the cramps are then to be removed, or the work must be left cramped up until the glue has set, and any pegs, nails or screws added then.

When should excess glue be removed?

Any excess glue squeezed out of joints must be removed while still wet. It is easy to remove at this stage with a wet cloth, but if left to set removal becomes difficult, and damage can be caused in the process.

If the work is to be given a clear finish, care must be used to remove every trace of glue. Failure to do this will result in patches being visible through the finish. This is because the glue seals the surface of the wood, and therefore changes the way in which absorption takes place which in turn affects the colour.

When should joggles be removed from the work?

Joggles and other excess wood deliberately left on at the time the joints are prepared are normally sawn off and levelled after assembly as part of the final cleaning-up. On joinery work, though, joggles are usually left on items like doors, and door and window frames, until they are actually fixed on the site. Joggles left on doors help to protect the door, and those on door and window frames are often used for building-in purposes.

111

9
Methods of finishing

What are the best methods of filling nail holes and small cracks prior to finishing?

The methods used depend on the job, and how it is to be finished. For painted woodwork, putty is quite satisfactory for small holes and cracks, or one of the multi-purpose plaster-based fillers can be used. The latter are available as powders requiring the addition of water, or in ready-prepared form in tubs and tubes.

For furniture-type projects, proprietary fillers, or 'stopping', provide a convenient method. These are available in small tins, and are made in a range of colours to match most of the typical wood shades. Stopping is made in interior and exterior grades. In use, the filler is well-pressed into the fault, left to dry, then the excess sanded and levelled off.

How can knots be prevented from exuding resin when the work is to be painted?

The usual way is to seal the knots by brushing over the area with a preparation known as 'knotting'. Knotting is a form of thick French polish, that is, shellac dissolved in alcohol, or methylated spirits, and is quick-drying. It is also claimed that certain types of aluminium priming paint are effective over resinous knots.

What are the basic stages of painting new wood?

The stages are as follows:

1. Ensure the work is properly prepared, and well cleaned to remove dust and loose particles. As far as possible, work in clean conditions, and avoid dust and draughts.
2. Apply a coat of priming paint, but do not leave any excess on the surface. Allow at least 12 hours to dry, and rub down lightly with fairly fine abrasive paper, grade 1 usually being about right. Rubbing-down is also known as 'flatting down', and 'de-knibbing', and is an essential part of most finishing processes. The purpose is to ensure the surface is always smooth.
3. Apply a coat of undercoating, colour-matched to the final shade required. Leave to dry, then rub down.
4. Apply a coat of gloss, or top coat. The final coat is not rubbed down, unless it is to be re-coated. For a gloss finish, a total of three coats are the minimum which need to be given. For extra quality and better wearing characteristics, either a second coat of undercoating, or an extra coat of gloss, can be given.

What is meant by 'laying-off', when applying paint?

Laying-off is the final brushing-over of the surface before leaving it to dry, and applies particularly to the final coat. All oil paints must be brushed very thoroughly, to ensure as even a distribution as possible. When laying-off, all the strokes are made in one direction to minimise brush marks, and help the final 'flow' of the paint film so that the surface is as free of blemishes as possible.

Care is needed not to drag the brush across the ends of the work, as this is a common cause of runs. Runs are also caused by overloading the brush, and then not brushing out sufficiently. On vertical surfaces, laying-off should also be carried out by vertical strokes, which also helps to reduce the risk of runs forming.

What are the main types of varnish?

The three main types of varnish are oil, shellac, and polyurethane. Oil varnishes are based on boiled linseed oil, are the traditional varnishes, and can be manufactured with slightly varying properties, for example, marine varnish for use on boats.

Shellac varnish, like knotting, is based on shellac and alcohol, and often has resins added to make it dry harder. It is quick-drying, but offers little resistance against either heat or moisture. Shellac varnish is also known as spirit varnish.

Polyurethane varnishes take advantage of modern technology, to provide a transparent film which is particularly tough and scratch-resisting, withstands reasonable temperatures, and is unaffected by most household liquids. In addition, these varnishes have exceptional qualities of flow, which means that with care surfaces almost entirely free of blemishes can be easily achieved.

What varieties of polyurethane varnish are available?

There are three varieties of this varnish, which give different degrees of shine to the final surface. They are (a) full gloss, (b) egg-shell, which is a semi-gloss, and (c) matt, which is non-glossy.

On most previously-untreated surfaces, a total of three coats is needed, with a minimum of two if the wood is fairly dense. Regardless of the final effect required, though, foundation coats must always be of the gloss variety. As with painting, rubbing-down between coats plays a most significant part in the quality of the results.

It is often recommended that the first coat applied when varnishing be diluted by up to 10 per cent with white spirit. This allows for better penetration into the wood, and therefore provides a better key.

What are the different types of stain available?

Most stains are made by dissolving dye, usually in the form of powder, in a liquid, this being called the solvent. Stains are

114

classified according to the solvent, the common ones being water, methylated spirits, naphtha, and ethanol.

Water stains are cheap, and give very even results, but are slow to dry. Spirit stains are quick-drying, but can give very patchy results unless considerable care is used. Naphtha stains are easy to apply, but are likely to leave dark deposits in the pores of the grain, and also tend to make end grain darker than the remaining surfaces. Ethanol stains give even, uniform colouring and are simple to apply.

Water and spirit stains are normally bought as powders and mixed in the workshop. Proprietary stains are usually ethanol-based, and are bought ready to apply. Stains can be intermixed within their own solvent group.

The effect of staining can also be achieved on certain woods by chemical action. Oak can be darkened by the application of ammonia, or preferably by exposure to ammonia fumes; permanganate of potash, although giving a reddish liquid when dissolved in water darkens the wood by chemical action.

How are stains applied?

Stains can be applied by brush, or by rag. However applied, though, it is advisable to give the surface a final rub over with a dry cloth, in order to absorb any excess and ensure an even distribution.

What is an oiled finish?

Oiling the wood to provide the finish is a method which dates back over 400 years. Until a few years ago, boiled linseed oil was used, this being one of the few oils which dries, although very slowly. It is applied fairly liberally, then rubbed vigorously by rag, this being repeated several times to build up the patina. Although linseed oil enhances the grain most attractively when newly applied, it only seals the surface to a very limited extent. This means that over a period of time dirt tends to become embedded in the grain, especially if this is of an open nature.

Oiling has now been updated, and the technique is now carried out using teak or Danish oil. These have better sealing qualities than has linseed, and also much improved drying characteristics. Oiled surfaces are only of a low sheen, and the method is used for furniture and hardwood joinery.

How is waxing carried out?

Waxing is another fairly simple, and very old, method of wood finishing. Genuine beeswax polish is made by dissolving pure beeswax in turpentine to give a soft consistency. This is then rubbed by rag onto the work, preferably working across the grain so as to drive the wax into the pores. It is then left for half an hour or so to allow the solvent to evaporate, then the surface is burnished vigorously by cloth to remove excess wax from the wood and impart the mellow sheen associated with waxing. For mouldings and similar uneven surfaces, the burnishing can be by brush, shoe-shine fashion. Waxing can be renewed and enlivened at any time, but this too is likely to become soiled over a period of time.

To lessen the risk of eventual soiling, and to provide a foundation for the wax, it is common practice to initially give the work a couple of coats of French polish. For light-coloured woods, this should be of white polish, otherwise slight discolouring will occur.

Is there a simple way of carrying out French polishing?

Yes, although the results inevitably fall well short of the excellent finishes which can be achieved when this polish is applied in expert manner in the traditional way by rubber.

The polish is applied by brush, or preferably using a polisher's mop. The best of these are made of squirrel hair, which as well as being soft has the property of evenly controlling the flow of polish onto the surface. As many as ten or 12 coats are given, as thinly as possible, with the surface lightly rubbed-down with flour paper between coats, but only when quite hard.

The work may be left directly from the final application by mop, when the level of shine should be fairly high. A more mellow effect can be imparted by rubbing over the surface in the direction of the grain with fine steel wool, grade 00 or finer. The steel wool should be dipped into wax polish first, which eliminates the risk of scratching, and adds to the final effect.

What are catalyst lacquers?

Catalyst or plastic lacquers are highly viscous, and set by chemical action once the catalyst is added. The usual ratio is one part of catalyst to 20 parts lacquer, and only enough must be mixed for immediate use. The mixed lacquer is applied as liberally as possible, and as the mixture does not rely on oxidisation or evaporation for hardening, setting is uniform and complete throughout the film.

Rubbing-down or flatting after coating must be complete and thorough, and this is carried out with wet-and-dry abrasive paper of 400 grade, and using water as the lubricant. Rubbing-down is continued until all traces of the original gloss have disappeared, and the surface has a uniform dullness. Two or three coats are applied and flatted in this way, the final lustre being obtained by rubbing with the burnishing cream supplied to suit the lacquer. A power drill with a polishing mop is useful for the burnishing stage. An egg-shell effect can be gained by rubbing-down with wire wool and wax after final burnishing.

Because of the thick coats which need to be applied with this lacquer, and the extensive flatting required, the lacquer is at its best when given to broad, horizontal surfaces. It is an ideal polish for table tops, is extremely tough and highly resistant to scratching, and to marking from hot objects and domestic liquids. Although both care and a great deal of rubbing are required, special skills are not needed and very excellent results can be obtained the first time this lacquer is used.

How can outdoor woodwork, such as garden sheds and fences, best be protected against rot?

Ideally, wood which is to be totally exposed to the elements should be pre-treated before use. This is a factory process, and timber properly treated becomes virtually rot-proof whether above or below the ground.

There are many proprietary preservatives which when applied to the timber act as both a water repellant and a rot preventative. They are normally brushed on, although particularly vulnerable items like fencing posts are best immersed for several days in the preservative. These preservatives are available either clear, or coloured, of which 'red cedar' is popular where the timber is to be left as treated. Most modern chemical preservatives can subsequently be painted in the usual way, once completely dry.

Can creosoted wood subsequently be painted?

No. The creosote tends to bleed through the paint, discolouring it and leaving an oily film on the surface. However, it is claimed that some aluminium-based paints act as an effective seal over creosote, but generally wood once treated with this preservative are best re-treated in the same way.

How are brushes used for finishing best cleaned?

Brushes should be immersed in a container of the same solvent as used for the finishing process, and agitated so as to swill out as much of the finishing medium as possible. They should then be dried on a piece of rag, followed by washing with soap and hot water. The bristles should be carefully 'shaped' before leaving to dry

Brushes with very soft hairs, such as polisher's mops, should be suspended in the solvent, rather than stood, as complete misshaping of the head can result.

Index